ROTTEN EVIDENCE

McSWEENEY'S
SAN FRANCISCO

Copyright © Ahmed Naji, 2019

First published as *Hirz mikamkim* by Sefsafa Publishing House, Giza, in 2019; second edition by Khan Aljanub, Berlin, in 2021. Translation © Katharine Halls, 2023.

McSweeney's and colophon are registered trademarks of McSweeney's, an independent publisher based in San Francisco.

ISBN: 978-1-952119-83-5

Cover art by Sophy Hollington

10 9 8 7 6 5 4 3 2 1

www.mcsweeneys.net

Printed in the United States

ROTTEN EVIDENCE

*Reading and Writing
in an Egyptian Prison*

AHMED NAJI

TRANSLATED BY
Katharine Halls

TIMELINE

AUGUST 2014: Tarek al-Taher, the editor in chief of *Literature Review* (*Akhbar al-Adab*), publishes an excerpt from Ahmed Naji's second novel, *Using Life*.

APRIL 2015: A sixty-five-year-old Egyptian man files a case against Naji, alleging that reading the excerpt caused him to experience palpitations, sickness, and a drop in blood pressure. Egyptian authorities open a case against Naji and al-Taher.

NOVEMBER 2015: Naji and al-Taher's case goes to trial. The prosecutor claims Naji's novel is a "malicious violation of the sanctity of morals."

JANUARY 2016: Naji and al-Taher are acquitted on charges of violating public decency. Prosecutors file an appeal shortly thereafter, arguing that Naji's text "harmed public morals." The appeal trial is set for February 6.

FEBRUARY 2016: An Egyptian higher court delivers a guilty verdict and imposes the maximum sentence of two years in prison for Naji. Also, al-Taher is fined for publishing the excerpt. The pair immediately appeal, but it is months before hearings get underway. In the meantime, Naji is taken straight to prison.

MARCH 2016: PEN America announces it will confer the PEN/Barbey Freedom to Write Award on Naji at its annual Literary Gala in New York.

AUGUST 2016: PEN America sends a letter, with the signatures of more than 120 writers, to Egyptian president 'Abd al-Fattah al-Sisi demanding Naji's immediate release.

DECEMBER 2016: Naji's prison sentence is suspended after he's served ten months in prison, and he is temporarily released but remains under a travel ban.

MAY 2017: A Cairo appeals court overturns the February 2016 decision, but also orders the case be retried.

MAY 2018: At the retrial, a Cairo criminal court lifts Naji's travel ban and overturns the original sentence, replacing his jail time with a fine of LE 20,000 ($1,130).

JULY 2018: Naji, finally able to leave Egypt, moves to the United States.

BEGINNINGS

I PICKED UP THE GREEN bag that held the clothes they'd permitted me to keep. In my other hand I carried a plastic bag of food, and under one arm was the blanket the intelligence lieutenant had allowed me—as a favor—to bring in with me. I kept tripping on the baggy pant legs of the coarse blue prison uniform. I was escorted by four plainclothes officers, while the lieutenant and another officer walked ahead of us.

I was behind them, but I was leading.

We passed through a small garden planted with a handful of trees and lots of cacti. In one corner was a carved wooden bust, poorly proportioned, of a person who was shackled at the wrists. He appeared to be writhing with indigestion. I glanced up at the building ahead of us: it was two stories high and painted a pale blue, and on the wall facing us was a mural depicting a lush equatorial landscape with a waterfall that cascaded all the way from the roof to ground level, then flowed sideways into a small brook that ran through a rainforest teeming with greenery and brightly colored flowers. The mural was remarkably pristine, except for where it was interrupted by windows or the metal door we were now walking toward. I stopped for a second to take in the incongruous sight: the last thing I'd expected to find in prison was a classic specimen of terrible tropical kitsch. The whole place was full of the kinds of printed wallpaper nature scenes that were fashionable in the '80s and '90s, but this masterpiece had been meticulously painted by the hand of an artist willing to deploy every last drop of their mawkish talent in an attempt to make the prison facility look cheerful.

It felt like a nightmare, not a prison; how else to explain these artistic flourishes that seemed custom-made to personally enrage and revolt me? Had the walls been a grim black or a dirty yellow, like public buildings usually are, it would never have aggravated me the way this silent tropical monstrosity did.

One of the plainclothes guys gave me a shove and we went in through the metal door. Another gentleman led me up to the first floor, and as we ascended, the stream of tacky shit followed us, in full color, along the walls: First, a sun setting behind a wooded hill topped with a European-looking log cabin; then another sunset, this time on a palm-lined beach. On it went; the only respite for the eyes was the occasional framed quotation from the Holy Qur'an. These lurid scenes were painted with a high degree of artistry: in one, for example, the rays of the setting sun filtered delicately through the branches of a tree, and you could clearly make out the careful brushstrokes where the painter had alternated between orange and green—indeed, had switched to a smaller brush to give the emerald leaves an incandescent golden outline. The proportions, depth, and perspective were, for the most part, highly accurate; to me, the mere fact that the paintings were three-dimensional was already impressive enough. It was certainly well-executed kitsch, even if it was hard on the eyes and the stomach. I tend to experience art viscerally—I feel it involuntarily in my digestive system, all the way down to my urinary tract—and the result can be pain, pleasure, or a cramp. Agony or delight. And all this was just a first taste of the torment that would be my daily bread here in Tura Agricultural Prison, where I was sentenced to spend two years for gross violation of public decency.

My image of prison was a cell that was isolated from the outside world. It would be gray; no other color could exist there. But when prison became my life, the things I'd imagined all seemed naive, like a collage I'd put together out of bits and pieces of prison literature and art. Instead, prison turned out to be painted in garish colors and decorated with the sort of European baroque landscapes that the modern Egyptian considered a tasteful addition to their sitting room or juice bar.

The state and the powers that be thought these bright colors would improve their standing in the field of human rights; they made the prison look nice for the carnivalesque media delegations that showed up every so often to set the record straight on the lies peddled by activists and foreign NGOs. On more than one occasion, in fact, the announcement of an official pardon for a few dozen prisoners would be the pretext for them to lock us all in our cells, then order the army conscripts who worked as sentries to put on civvies and impersonate the pardoned inmates in the garden. The external gates would open, and reporters and TV cameras would stream in to film the "prisoners" who had supposedly been granted a reprieve against a backdrop of desert-island beaches and Scandinavian pine forests. The soldiers obediently danced and laughed for the cameras and prostrated themselves in the dust, raising their hands in prayer and gratitude for the mercy and generosity and kindheartedness of the president and the minister of the interior.

Even the isolation that I'd imagined would accompany the gray color didn't turn out to exist. When the guard closed the cellblock door, I found myself in a space designed for sixty prisoners that actually held many more. Some people were lying on the floor, in the bathroom, or in the kitchen. I was led straight to an upper bunk. The bunks were concrete ledges, eighty centimeters long and thirty centimeters wide. I spent the first hour being stared at by my cellmates—they were pretty taken aback at the sight of the chief of intelligence personally leading me into the cellblock and choosing a bunk for me—and then found myself obliged to pray with them, drink tea, smile, ask and answer questions, and generally perform the standard rituals of social integration.

There was going to be no escape from society here in prison, clearly. Still, with the nuisance of social niceties came a sense of fellowship and welcome. One young man came over to take my bags and wipe down my bunk with a wet rag, while another offered me a seat on his own bunk. A third made me a cup of tea, and a fourth offered me a cigarette. When the first man had finished cleaning my bunk, he took my blanket, folded it in two lengthwise, and carefully laid it out so I could sleep between the two halves; it was still only February, and at that time of year the cold and the damp went straight to your bones. "I made you a sandwich," he said with a grin.

"He's good at making the bed, that one," said another cellmate, to a round of laughter. *Making the bed* was teenage slang for "making out"; I hadn't heard this kind of banter, full of innuendo and in-jokes, since high school. But in the company of over sixty other males, it was to be the central feature of all communication. No mention of "making the bed" could pass without provoking a stream of allusions to hanky-panky and heavy petting. Even the most straightforward remarks, like "Here, take this," would invite crude comments like "Take it where?," leaving the cellblock in fits of laughter. The language I'd been imprisoned for using was standard fare inside prison, along with good old Egyptian poor taste. *Give us our due, O Lord of the Heavens; grant it to whom you will and absolve or debase whom you please...*

I never tried to change society, except for a brief period as a child when I dreamed I was the long-awaited Messiah—which I later found out was a fairly common fantasy among Muslim children. I never had an all-encompassing vision of life, or of anything that might qualify me to teach or guide others, or even to really annoy them. I wrote a novel about my own sense of alienation; about the friends I loved, the ones that didn't love me back, and the ones that loved me even though I didn't think I deserved all that love; about the city that swallowed up my best years and turned me into an arrogant, ignorant prick. I never took part in any political struggles. It wasn't the Muslim Brotherhood or the Salafists or some religious fundamentalist movement that took me to court and accused me of offending public morality: it was an educated citizen and a lawyer, no less, in concert with another, even less significant citizen who happened to be a journalist. And it was the public prosecution office, a bastion of the justice system, that enthusiastically took up the case against me and appealed when the court of first instance found me innocent. The party whose morality was offended was the very authority that claimed to be secular. They wielded the fires of hell in one hand and the torch of enlightenment in the other.

NO BOOKS

A SENIOR POLICE OFFICER WEARING a major's epaulets flicked through the books in my bag. I was naked except for boxers, and surrounded by plainclothes detectives and regular guards from both the prison and the police precinct I'd just come from. These rituals marked my handover from precinct to prison. At the prison gate I'd been ordered to strip for inspection in front of the welcome party, then left to stand in the sun while they signed the paperwork and went through every scrap of fabric in my duffel bag with no sense of urgency. Finally, someone handed me a pair of blue pants and a blue shirt with the word INMATE written on the back.

The major—later I found out he was the prison's chief of intelligence—picked two books out of my bag: Patrick Modiano's *Des inconnues*, translated by Rana Hayek; and Almog Behar's *Chahla ve-Hezkel* in Nael Eltoukhy's translation. He shook his head. "I can't let you bring these in unless they've been approved by National Security. They'll have to be left in Property. There's a library; you can read the books there." Then he picked up the black leather notebook I used for jotting down thoughts, journal entries, and sometimes notes for my journalism.

"I know you're a writer and all that," he said in a conspiratorial whisper. "So I'll let you keep your journal and your pens."

I managed a muttered "thank you" in among the nervous stammering coming out of my mouth. I don't think I said more than three words during the inspection: *okay*, *sir*, and *thanks*. I was exhausted after three days of sleeping on the tiled floor in the precinct. Exhausted from the journey to the prison in the back of a filthy metal van. From the tension, from the simultaneous hunger and lack of appetite, from the worry and fear, from the humiliation and abuse, from finding myself thrust suddenly into a battle I hadn't chosen.

Not long after I arrived in cellblock 2/4, once the young men had greeted me and prepared my bunk, one of my cellmates suggested I take a shower. I hadn't washed in over four days; we hadn't been allowed to at the precinct. In the shower stall, I pulled the dirty curtain closed behind me, shrinking away from the walls, where cockroaches and assorted other insects roamed, and turned on the water. It was the most incredible shower I'd taken in my life. After the privations of prison, the simplest comfort feels like the pleasures of this world and the next combined.

I left the bathroom, headed for my bunk, and fell asleep. When I woke up, evening life was well underway in the cellblock. Groups of inmates were gathered around contraband games like chess and cards, while others stood in front of the television watching an old show. Only five channels of state television were available to us, and it was up to the prisoners to decide what to watch. There were a few exceptions to this, however. The guards mandated that we show the occasional presidential speech, the 9:00 p.m. news, and football matches. You could choose not to look at the screen, but they'd still blare through the cellblock at full volume.

Lights-out was at midnight exactly, by which time the chess players and cardplayers had thinned out. Prisoners had to remain in their bunk all night other than to go to the bathroom. Glancing down at the bunk below mine, I could see my cellmate was reading Jehan Sadat's *A Woman of Egypt* by the light of a bulb connected to bare wires stuck straight into a socket in the wall. I tossed and turned in my blanket sandwich, wide-awake. My downstairs neighbor closed the book. Very politely and timidly, I asked if I could take a look. He smiled and handed it to me, then adjusted his jerry-rigged bedside lamp—which had half of an old plastic bleach bottle fitted around it to make a lampshade—so it shone in my direction.

I spent the night engrossed in the former First Lady's auto-biography, reading about her kind heart, her brilliant intelli-gence, her struggle to gain an education, her efforts to cultivate her husband by inviting intellectuals and writers to lunches and Ramadan breakfasts, her charitable works, her tireless efforts on behalf of war victims, her role in changing the country's personal status laws, and her distress at the unfair aspersions and baseless accusations that were regularly cast against her. It was a good book for a first night in prison—full of lies, exaggerations, gossip, and name-dropping about her warm relations with various heads of state and their wives, from Shaykha Fatima of the United Arab Emirates to Colonel Gadhafi's wife—and sometime around dawn, I finally drifted into sleep.

When I woke up the next morning, I grabbed my black notebook and jotted down what I could remember of my dream. One bunk over, I spotted another book, small and old, with an illustration of the writer Taha Hussein on its battered cover and the title *With Abu al-'Ala' al-Ma'arri in His Prison*. I smiled and looked ceilingward, appreciating the auspicious sign. Coincidences don't mean anything, not rationally, but you can't help giving them some credence. Someone out there is thinking of you. Someone is whispering your name; you haven't been forgotten yet.

In the introduction to the book (which I kept, by the way, when I got out of prison), Taha Hussein talks about his personal relationship with the famed poet of the city of Ma'arrat al-Nu'man. He'd studied al-Ma'arri early in his academic career, but this exquisite book came decades later—like he was returning to his first love—after a summer holiday in France with his family, when he decided to take al-Ma'arri along for company. In the book he re-reads his favorite verses, and takes us on a journey into al-Ma'arri's three prisons, as Hussein puts it: the prison of his blindness; the prison of his house, which he never left; and the prison of the body that stifles the soul. Hussein comments that al-Ma'arri spent his career imprisoning himself ever more firmly, setting constraints that didn't need to be met: where most poets held themselves captive to one rhyme scheme, he forced himself to incorporate two, an even more complex formal challenge.

Unlike other poets of the medieval period, al-Ma'arri wasn't tempted to make the move to Baghdad to write praise poetry for princes and shaykhs or compose odes to singing girls. Instead, he stayed home dueling the ghosts of metaphysics and taking on the merchants of religion and morality. In his work he never attempted to reach out to others or send a message to the unfaithful; he never asked anyone to join his cause or rebel against the contradictions of religion, fantasy, and human morality. He was a nihilist: life, to al-Ma'arri, was dust and more dust, and nothing had any value but his commitments as an artist, his total immersion in language and literature, and his endless preoccupation with arranging and rearranging letters and words. This burning desire kept the darkness at bay in the prison al-Ma'arri had built for himself.

In Hussein's book, the literary analysis is frequently interrupted by observations of the French train stations he passes through, or the gentle breeze blowing across the European seashore; every so often his attention abruptly turns to a painting by Degas or a text by Paul Valéry, like this one, which, when I read it, felt like it had been dedicated to me: "Après tout, la vie de quelqu'un n'est qu'une suite de hasards, et de réponses plus ou moins exactes à ces événements quelconques..." "After all, a person's life is no more than a series of coincidences, and of more or less direct responses to these random events..."

Written as Hussein relaxed on sandy French beaches, the book skips back and forth between self-deprecating remarks—and remarks deprecating Arab society—and his discussion of al-Ma'arri. Hussein warns more than once that the book isn't a work of literary criticism but a diversion, the result of a mind taking pleasure in the company of a friend from another era. It wasn't actually that pleasant to read, though—not right at the beginning of my time in prison—and instead plunged me into a morass of miserable thoughts. I beat myself up hourly for getting myself into this mess. Why did you do this, Ahmed? I'd ask accusingly as I showered in the company of the cockroaches scuttling across the walls. Did you really have to write that stuff? Are the fantasies you chase after in your writing really worth this sacrifice? I never took myself or what I did seriously; I was just messing around, killing time. How had the game suddenly gone too far, without me ever sensing the danger?

In July, five months after my arrival, when the heat and humidity in prison ate at our skin, two books arrived from my close friend Ahmed Wael: a rare copy of the diwan of Rashid ibn Ishaq al-Katib, known as Abu Hakima, in an edition by Muhammad Husayn al-A'raji, and Taha Hussein's *The Future of Culture in Egypt*. I was literally rotting, my body permanently oozing sweat, when I reached the final chapters of the Hussein, in which he sends a simultaneously veiled and not-so-veiled message to the security services and public prosecution office before whom he himself had once stood accused of apostasy.

> How often are our writers criticized for only taking an interest in the surface aspect of beings, without depicting their inward natures or plumbing their innermost depths, not a trace of which appears in their work. But let them do what they are reproached for neglecting to do, let them display the human soul denuded as their European peers do; trust that they are capable of doing so and capable indeed of excelling therein, of distinguishing themselves if they try. Let them do all that: then witness the animosity that will be turned against them by the public, men of religion, security services, and public prosecution office.

I for one was very cautious, Dr. Hussein. I figured these things out in my early days of writing, when I was first becoming acquainted with the historical lineage I seemingly belonged to. I tried as best I could to say what I wanted to say, then found some circuitous way to set it down in print: sometimes I used a pen name, sometimes I shared my writings with friends and no one else, and sometimes I just kept them in the pages of my diary. Many writers in Egypt choose an ivory tower of sorts: they write detached, convoluted, academic prose that speaks to their fellow writers. This path isn't chosen out of arrogance or vanity but out of the writer's fear of acknowledging the secrets inside themselves, and of the risks of releasing them into the world. The dilemma, as Hussein put it, was this:

> Writers in our country are not free, whether in relation to the state or to their readers. So much exceptional talent goes to waste because it suppresses itself, forcing itself not to engage in creation out of fear of the state, or out of fear of readers, because in our country there are subjects which might occur to writers that the law won't stand for, the regime won't tolerate, and popular tastes won't welcome.

Hussein wrote these words in 1938, elated at the conclusion of the Anglo-Egyptian Treaty of 1936. It seemed to him that Egypt had finally gained independence; his book was a manifesto, a program for the regeneration and refinement of education and cultural life in Egypt. In this moment, Hussein was giving up his isolation, his claim to exceptional talent, and even his own desires, to serve his readers and his country. A once-spurned prophet who could foresee the future, he held a lantern overhead in an attempt to guide his people through the darkness, toward enlightenment and progress.

Day 6: Friday, February 26, 2016

Slept deeply last night, didn't want to wake up. There's no recreation on Fridays and the cell isn't opened at all. Inmates aren't allowed to go to the mosque to listen to the sermon given by the ass-licking state-appointed preacher; instead, his voice blasts through the PA, vituperating against the diabolical Muslim Brotherhood and their cheap abuse of religion, and praying for triumph and the success of the country's leaders.

I found that my cellmates had spread their prayer mats out in the passageway. One man, a former officer in the Republican Guards, stepped forward to take up the role of prayer leader, clutching a sheaf of papers bearing the sermon he'd written himself.

The former Republican Guard (who'd been charged with theft and leaking confidential documents) cleared his throat with a round of "bismillahs," then launched into a sermon so uniformly ungrammatical and badly pronounced that it was painful to listen to. It was all the worse because he'd hardly chosen an uncontroversial topic: from cellblock 2/4 of Tura Agricultural Prison, our officer-turned-prisoner had taken it upon himself to rebut Western accusations that the Prophet was a philanderer and a sex addict, by defending polygamy and offering a detailed justification for each of the Prophet's marriages. The stupidity of his arguments and his abominable articulation and delivery had me feeling near suicidal. Every time he attempted to recite a hadith or an ayah from the Qur'an, the words came tumbling out of his mouth like the letters themselves had tripped over one another.

PISSING IN A BOTTLE

THEY BROUGHT A CHAIR INTO my detention cage. It was that time around midday when the police station was quiet and not much went on. I took out my Modiano novel and was reading when the lieutenant stormed in, yelling, "Get your stuff now! There's an inspection coming any minute and we need you out of here!"

I put the small plastic bags that contained my possessions into larger plastic bags. I was let out of the cage, and the lieutenant dragged me outside to the police van, confiscating my mobile phone, which he'd let me use for the last few days. This lieutenant was one of the nicer ones, so I believed what he said and complied peaceably with his orders. "You lie low in here until the inspectors have gone," he said, feigning a conspiratorial kindness.

The van had a large blue-painted metal cargo box, like the kind used for transporting Central Security soldiers—our local riot police. I got into the empty box alone, and the door slammed shut behind me. Then suddenly the van roared to life and pulled away and I understood the trick.

They'd gotten what they wanted: I was being taken to prison, after three days' detention at the police station. They'd made it a surprise so I couldn't ask for help and nobody would know. The journey took around an hour and a half; alone in the large space, I jolted back and forth with every bump in the road, hitting the metal walls of the cargo box left and right, up and down. Every movement made me more acutely aware of the pressure on my bladder, which was beginning to hurt, and of the rotten-egg smell that filled the air. The floor of the box was covered in garbage, mud, plastic bags, and empty fizzy-drink bottles. I picked one up, unscrewed the lid, pulled my pants down, and pointed the tip of my penis into the mouth, where it released a stream of dark yellow urine.

My nerves and muscles relaxed with a deep sense of relief, and I felt a haze lifting from my mind. I didn't want to show up with a full bladder. I knew even then that once you arrive in prison, you never know when they'll let you piss.

Day 2: Monday, February 22, 2016

Bulaq police station. The old Bulaq hammam, one of the few public hammams still in use today—men splashing around in wet boxer shorts—is just a few meters from here. There's also the Bawaki district, which was the most important market in Cairo and the entire Middle East until the nineteenth century. Goods arrived here from the other Egyptian provinces, from the north, and from lands in the east. The police station's probably been in this same spot the whole time.

It gets quieter in the police station at night, and nocturnal creatures appear. A clutch of tiny kittens comes out to play and tries to steal my food, and a weasel vanishes and reappears as it darts from room to room.

THE NABATSHI REGIME

I'D BARELY CLIMBED UP TO my bunk on my first day, when a man came over and introduced himself as the nabatshi's deputy. The nabatshi, he said, gesturing to a white-haired man, was the head honcho in the cellblock.

The nabatshi's dues consisted of three packs of cigarettes, to be paid to the deputy or the nabatshi himself. This sum covered the daily cleaning of the cellblock, plus maintenance and repairs. There were other dues related to meals. You could choose one of two prisoners to cook for you: one required you to go to the prison cafeteria to purchase your own ingredients, which he'd then cook in exchange for two packs of cigarettes; the other asked you to deposit a certain sum in your cafeteria account, which he would use to purchase the ingredients he needed, and likewise take two packs of cigarettes for himself.

After lights-out at midnight, the TV was muted, and its silent screen would continue to cast a colored glow across the darkened cell until 1:00 a.m.

There were two refrigerators. You could use them to store any frozen food you'd been given on visits, excluding cooked rice or pasta dishes. Meat was also stored in the refrigerators, which were opened twice a day: at 1:00 p.m., when the daily ration of protein—red meat or chicken—was doled out, and again in the early evening, so those fasting could have their meal after sunset.

The nabatshi was chosen by the chief of intelligence. A number of factors influenced the selection: the candidate had to enjoy the trust of the chief of intelligence, of course, and be capable of commanding the prisoners in his cellblock. Nabatshi dues varied from one cellblock to another. In my first cell it was three packs of cigarettes, but when I was transferred to a classier block—known as the Pashas—it was five, since standards of cleanliness and organization there were supposedly higher. In the second cellblock, not all five toilets were available for general use. Several stalls were reserved for those who paid an extra pack of cigarettes each week; their names were posted on the door to the WC. These five-star stalls contained European seated toilets—as opposed to squat toilets, which were essentially just holes in the ground—and were cleaned twice a day with bleach powder.

These precise regimes were developed by prisoners to make life under prison conditions, and under the unpredictable tyranny of the guards, more bearable. Thanks to this ingenuity—and the familiarity, understanding, and solicitude with which I was welcomed by the residents of cellblock 2/4—I settled into the rhythm of daily life in prison within a week. The days were like a wheel that turned, following the same arc at a pace that never changed.

I would wake up between ten and eleven in the morning. On good days, there would be enough water pressure to power the refreshing trickle that counted for a shower, and if I was especially lucky, the water would be warm. After washing, I'd change my underwear and get dressed. From a plastic bag I'd hung on the wall, I'd take some bread and cheese. I'd empty a packet of Nescafé into my plastic cup, then borrow an electric kettle belonging to a cellmate and add hot water. I'd stir my Nescafé and chew at the cheese sandwich until the cellblock was unlocked, at 12:30 p.m.

We had one hour for recreation. I'd usually use this time to exchange books at the library, but some days I'd stroll around the walkway instead, shaking out my body as best I could, or hunting out the areas where sunlight had made it through the bars that covered the internal courtyard. When I found one, I'd roll up my sleeves, or go ahead and take my shirt off if there were no guards around, and stand topless, bathing myself in sunshine in an attempt to get some vitamin D. Sometimes I'd play sports with my cellmates. In truth, there was only one sport, table tennis; we always played doubles, because with only one table and a limited amount of time, there was no way enough people would get a turn otherwise.

After rec was the time for reading the newspapers. The authorities allowed each prisoner to subscribe to a specified selection of papers; in my case, they agreed only to *al-Akhbar* and *al-Masri al-Yawm*. The prison officers always checked the papers before passing them to us, which is why they didn't arrive until after recreation hour. At some point, after reading a few pages of the newspaper, I'd get up and begin my search for the coffeepot. Making coffee remained a challenge until my girlfriend, Yasmine, was able to send me a bag containing clothes, underwear, food, cheese, coffee, and a coffeepot. These all found their way past the guards without any trouble, since Yasmine had addressed them to my cellmate, who was subject to fewer restrictions. When I finally unpacked the bag, I found a piece of paper stuck to a T-shirt that bore the words I LOVE YOU.

After I'd fixed coffee, I'd sit on my bunk and re-read Yasmine's last letter, or letters from friends that had managed to make their way to me. Then I'd go back to the newspapers, listlessly riffling through them until I got to the most interesting page: the one containing the sudoku and the crossword. I was hopeless at crosswords and puzzles until I went to prison—I didn't even know how sudoku worked—but I left prison as the cellblock sudoku champion and a serious crossword addict.

Dinner was at 5:00 or 6:00 p.m. After eating, I'd lie on my bunk tossing and turning, sometimes dozing and sometimes not. I'd get up again at 7:00 p.m. and begin pacing the cell, smoking cigarettes and trying to enthuse myself about whatever bullshit my cellmates were discussing; usually we swapped stories and anecdotes to pass the time. Soon it was time for the daily soap opera, which we watched on our cell's old TV. Sometimes I'd get bored of it and retreat to my bunk to read. When the lights went out at midnight, I'd switch on the "bedside lamp" I'd purchased two weeks in and continue to read.

In those early days, I did my best to stick to this routine no matter what. I also made absolutely sure never to pity myself or bemoan my fate, even in the most private corners of my mind.

Day 41: Friday, April 1, 2016

Right now we have two cellmates who are on trial in the same case. Yesterday things heated up—it started with backbiting and insinuations, and quickly descended into curses and punches. The others had to intervene to separate them. Everything settled down again after that, but we begged the nabatshi not to tell the authorities; otherwise, one or both would be punished. He refused outright, on the grounds that the authorities would find out through one of the birdies anyway, and his position didn't give him a choice about the matter.

Today they were both summoned to the administration. The one who threw the first punch was told he'd have to leave the cellblock and move downstairs to the felons' block. He's the one I borrow *al-Gumhuriyya* newspaper from every day, and on Saturdays the "Tears of Regret" supplement.

BIRDIES

I WAS A NEWBIE, SO as soon as the deputy nabatshi started telling me how the system worked, what the rates were, and when they were due, I whipped out my notebook and started taking notes. I recorded all my observations in that notebook—in code, so that if someone found it, they wouldn't understand anything—as well as all the new vocabulary I was learning. One of the first words I jotted down was *birdie*.

The cramped, overcrowded cell didn't have much room for bags and suitcases, which soon piled up chaotically, and it wasn't always easy to get hold of nails to make hooks in the walls: nails were a banned item because they could be turned into weapons. So the alternative was to make a birdie. You took a length of cord, or braided some leftover fabric into a rope, and looped it around one of the bars over the window, then fastened it to a disposable razor so the head of the razor formed a hook where you could hang a couple of things.

There were also more advanced survival techniques that you learned with time. For example, food went bad very quickly when stored in plastic bags hanging from a birdie, because the cellblock was sweaty and airless; with fruit in particular, you had to make sure it was dry on the surface; otherwise, it would mold within a matter of hours. Fruit and vegetables couldn't be stored in the fridge, which was reserved for protein foodstuffs, so the best method was to wrap each individual piece of fruit or vegetable in newspaper and store it in a plastic bag that had been pierced in several places with a pen to create ventilation holes.

The term *birdie* also designated something else: a snitch who passed on information about cellblock goings-on, down to every last whisper, to the prison intelligence. In other prisons, and indeed in other cellblocks, there weren't always so many birdies. Typically, prisoners convicted of violent or drug-related offenses, referred to as "felons," were separated from those convicted of run-of-the-mill bribery or embezzlement, of whom there were many, and these felons didn't like birdies. In the cell right next to ours, which housed felons exclusively—most of them murderers or drug dealers—they broke every rule in prison. The lights and TV stayed on all night, and they did whatever they felt like; they managed to have cell phones smuggled in, and drugs of various kinds. Prison authorities would regularly search the cell from top to bottom and yet never find what they were looking for, thanks to a pact of honor that existed among the felons. Birdies were not welcome there, and any that found their way in would be swiftly uncovered and dealt with at an opportune moment according to the conventions of cellblock justice. The electricity would cut out suddenly, and there'd be a resounding cry of "Cover your faces!," followed by a single scream that meant the birdie had gotten his face slashed with a shiv. Sometimes the felons were more lenient, and rather than scarring the birdie's face, they'd attack him in the shower and slash his butt cheeks instead; but still, he'd bear the mark of his betrayal forever.

In my cellblock, though—which was home to businessmen, bosses, deputy ministers, and other classy types—loyalty to the powers that be was firm and enduring (just as you would expect from a bunch of middle-class prisoners). They competed in kissing ass and in demonstrating obedience and allegiance, showering the guards with gifts of imported cigarettes and elaborate, defamatory gossip about everything occurring in the cellblock. All this would earn them five minutes more than their cellmates at visiting time, or the right to bring in a fan or an electric kettle, or maybe even just a small coffeepot—also on the banned-items list, because it was sturdy and made of metal and could be used without much difficulty to injure or to kill.

Day 34: Friday, March 25, 2016

At least here I can go to the bathroom when I want. When I was in the precinct, I had to wait for the right moment, then beg the cadet on duty to open the cell.

Found a book in the library: the Arabic translation of Robert Solé's *L'Égypte, passion française*, which recounts the expedition of Horace Vernet and Frédéric Goupil-Fesquet to Egypt in 1839. Armed with the strange contraption known as a photographic camera, they aimed to document the Orient and the wonders of pharaonic Egypt. To obtain permission to do so, they were obliged to meet the viceroy, Mehmet Ali Pasha, and they offered to take his photo, too, but he declined, fearing that the camera would snatch away his soul. Instead, they came to the agreement that the pair would accompany him to his palace and take a landscape photograph, while the viceroy sat to one side and observed their sorcery.

Back then, taking photos was a lengthy process: the exposure time could be half an hour, and then it had to be developed. Mehmet Ali sat watching warily, his hand resting on the hilt of his sword the whole time. When the image finally appeared, he took one look at it and said, "This is the work of the devil!" before turning on his heel and withdrawing to his chambers.

ALL LIBRARIES
LOOK THE SAME

AS FAR AS I WAS CONCERNED, the library of Taha Hussein
Public Secondary School for Boys—a squat building in Sandub,
in the city of al-Mansura—was in large part responsible for
the trouble I was in. It was the first state school I'd attended
after a roundabout excursion through the private schools of
Egypt and Kuwait, where I spent my childhood. Its buildings,
lavatories, and administrative procedures resembled less those
of a school than of a low-security prison, and in fact my abiding
image of all public and governmental institutions belonging to
the Egyptian state was profoundly shaped by my time at Taha
Hussein Secondary. The toilets reeked of body odor, the rooms
and corridors were poorly ventilated, and sticky, hot air groped
at you from every direction. Our classrooms looked out over a
graveyard. In front of that, just beyond the wall of the school
compound, was a fetid agricultural drainage ditch with a thin

layer of moldy-looking algae on the surface that swarmed with insects, to the musical accompaniment of frogs and grasshoppers, which we called "night cockroaches." My only escape from the ambient ignorance and filth was the library.

Since the school's establishment in the 1960s, the library had accumulated the complete works of Naguib Mahfouz, Tawfiq al-Hakim, Mustafa Mahmoud, and Anis Mansur, as well as the translated plays of Shakespeare, alongside shelves full of psychology and philosophy books. It was there that I first read the works of Freud and Nietzsche and the many other books that shaped my knowledge and understanding of myself and of life. A few were books it would have been impossible to read at any other age: I can hardly see myself picking up Mahfouz's long and slightly fusty Cairo trilogy, for example, as an adult. Others were gems I went back and searched for years later, like one foreign novel whose title had been translated into Arabic as *Sirwal al-Qiss,* or *The Priest's Pantaloons*, in which an upstanding priest finds himself washed up in a nudist colony inhabited by freethinkers, setting the stage for a battle between virtue and bodily freedom. Thanks to the internet, I found out the book in question was *The Bishop's Jaegers* by the American author Thorne Smith, and had been translated—like most of the other foreign-language titles I'd read—by Tharwat Okasha.

In prison, we weren't allowed out into the courtyard downstairs; we spent recreation in the walkways that ran between the cells on our floor. The second floor had four cellblocks, which were opened in turn for one hour each. Next to the stairs was a ping-pong table; the stairs themselves led down to the next floor or up to a single room that served as the library. The moment I stepped across the threshold, I felt like I'd returned to my high school library, the only difference being that the readers seated there were old men in white or blue uniforms. The wooden tables and chairs were exactly the same type we'd had at school; even the walls were painted the same color. The shelves were lined with the titles I'd read as a teenager: the complete works of al-Hakim and Mahfouz, a scattered few by Taha Hussein himself, the same green edition of Gamal al-Ghitani's *Zayni Barakat* that I'd borrowed from the school library, and of course the complete works of Anis Mansur. The only difference was that the inside cover of these bore not the words *Taha Hussein Public Secondary School* but the stamp of the Prisons Authority.

The books were mainly Ministry of Culture editions of various vintages, many from the '60s, but there were also titles published in the '70s by the Armed Forces Morale Affairs Department, including numerous collections of poetry by unheard-of female poets. These were all about their love for the nation and a handsome dark-skinned soldier, whom they implored to rescue them from some obscure pain and to win back their land and their honor. Then there were publications by Dar al-Shuruq, which of all the non-state publishing houses had the biggest share of shelf space in the prison library. And in the far corner was the religion section, which held three shelves of Christian books and an entire wall of Islamic literature. The selection of titles was a greatest hits that ranged from Qur'anic exegeses by Egypt's favorite cassette-tape preacher, Shaykh Sha'rawi; to the offerings of the Saudi Ministry of Islamic Affairs, including volumes of Ibn Taymiyya, Ibn Kathir, and Ibn Qayyim al-Jawziyyah, and all the other reading material a young terrorist-in-the-making might need. We hadn't had any of those in the school library, thank God, but here in prison they were obviously in the right place.

The man in charge of the library was a civilian employee who left promptly at two in the afternoon. He did little actual work, and instead two elderly inmates took care of the borrowing register (books could be borrowed for one day at a time) and inventoried the collection once every three months.

The newspapers and TV channels had covered my case intensively in the days prior to my arrival, so I was a familiar face, and I constantly found myself being smiled at and greeted by name by people I didn't know. One day as I was staring at the library shelves, an inmate in white—meaning he was pretrial and hadn't yet been sentenced—came up to me and introduced himself as the holder of a doctorate from al-Azhar University in one of the fields of religion. I nodded cordially, and he said he'd like to ask me a question, if I had time.

"We're in prison," I replied. "We have nothing but time."

"Well," he started, "I read an article by Dr. Ayman al-Gindi in *Egypt Today* that said what you wrote doesn't count as literature, and that you used language that really was offensive to public morality."

"Um, who's Dr. Ayman al-Gindi?"

"You've never heard of him?"

"I'm not very well-informed, I'm afraid."

"Thing is, he was saying—"

"Sorry," I cut in, "but I don't really want to talk about this."

"But—"

"Please, I mean it. I'm already in prison. I don't want to sit here listening to you repeating whatever swear words I supposedly used. Leave me alone, brother. I don't feel like talking to you."

I'd raised my voice. I was angry. He hurried off, almost tripping over himself in embarrassment. I turned toward the books lining the shelves, facing away from the civilian librarian and the other prisoners, and for the first time, I began to cry. It wouldn't be the last.

Day 5: Thursday, February 25, 2016

Melting of boredom in my bunk. Reading Ali Bader's *Papa Sartre*, wish it would go on forever. I take my time chewing over each page, because getting to the end will make the dead weight of boredom on my chest even heavier, and the slow passing of time even slower.

I think about an amazing ass, the most beautiful ass I've ever seen. I miss sex and I can't even find anywhere to masturbate. This morning one guy banged on the toilet door and yelled at the people inside, "Enough wanking, boys. You'll block the pipes!"

Love and loved ones recede into the distance. I train my memory by writing and recording names. My dreams are consoled by hope. I imagine everyone on holiday with me in Sinai, sitting down to a meal: all the people I love, on a sandy seashore, eating and laughing together, with no trace of rancor or bad feeling.

The one weakness I'm trying to get a grip on here is my temper. Losing control over your nerves or your composure has disastrous consequences. You don't want to find yourself in solitary.

There's an angry poet sitting on the tip of my nose.

This afternoon at roll call, a grim-faced police officer came in. His eyes were fixed on me the whole way down the walkway. I stared back, deliberately hostile and expressionless. He obviously thought I was a draft dodger, because he asked in an aggressive tone, "Soldier?"

"No," I replied.

"What's your name?"

"Ahmed."

"Sentenced?"

"Yes, two years."

"What do you do for a living?"

"I'm a journalist."

He nodded dismissively and walked off.

THE MASK

SKILLFUL SOCIAL DISSIMULATION REQUIRES KEEPING to yourself any opinions that might reveal your class status, political views, or religious inclination. It requires using only the most clichéd and socially neutral formulations in response to questions asked or gestures offered, along with platitudes like "That's how it goes," "The Lord is generous," and "God give you strength." It's a mask: you put on a calm smile and feign affection, good nature, and acceptance of whatever bullshit the other person's spouting, regardless of how vitriolic, stupid, or bigoted it is. Grin and take it as a joke; act dumb and pretend you haven't noticed how despicable it is. I've always been a masterful deployer of the mask: I can handle virtually any social situation that comes up, and I don't struggle to perform in public or adapt to unfamiliar environments.

The mask really proved its worth in prison. It earned me the respect and liking of inmates and guards, but wearing it for so long felt heavy, much heavier than usual. It weighed on my heart and soul, and added to the misery of waiting for time to pass. During my early days in prison, when I was reading was the only time I could take off the mask. I made a point of giving short, distracted, lifeless answers to anyone who interrupted me, to let them know that when I had my head in a book, I just wasn't there.

Being on a top bunk was a real pain in the ass. Unlike those of the residents of the lower bunks, my every movement was on view, and my possessions hung in plastic bags from nails on the wall for all to see. I knew I'd been put there so the birdies could keep an eye on me. Anything I said, anything I did, anyone I talked to, when I went to the toilet and how long I spent there, even what I read—it all got passed on to the administration via multiple sources. But behind my book, their surveillance couldn't get to me. Inside my book, I met people with whom I didn't need to pretend; we could talk seriously and harshly to one another; we could argue; we could imagine alternative histories and parallel worlds.

One day I looked up from my book to find a surprised cell-mate shaking me gently. "It's only your first week!" he said. "And you're already talking to yourself?"

FREE PROVOCATION

DESPITE EGYPT'S RAPID GROWTH IN population, which has just crossed the hundred million mark, the ability of its inhabitants to distinguish humans from animals appears to be decreasing. Anyone or anything free that refuses to assimilate into the general national lunacy is seen as being provocative. For the state, that makes you a dangerous saboteur; for society, it makes you an attention-seeker who's mildly entertaining at best.

Day 8: Sunday, February 28, 2016

Woke up in the middle of a dream to deafening noise. The plainclothes guy on nabatshi duty today is the most obnoxious one of the lot. In the morning, he comes in yelling and banging on a tin can. He sounds like an animal. I opened my eyes but lay still in my bunk, trying to preserve the rhythm of my breathing to stop myself from getting too furious. I felt a Hannibal-esque urge to tie the guard to a chair, open up his head, cook his brain in front of him, and then feed it to him in little pieces. I'd happily eat some of it myself.

The lower classes judge the characters of those around them by the values of generosity, manliness, and integrity; from the middle class upward, it's a person's appearance, the brands they wear, and their purchasing power that count. Here on the cellblock the difference between these class values is stark. I'm especially struck by the generous, affectionate treatment I get from the guys who are in for desertion. One of them, who came from my hometown, told me it was my father who circumcised him when he was a boy. My dad was always his favorite doctor, apparently. He's imposed his protection on me, and every few hours he shows up with some gift or other, insisting that I mustn't embarrass him by refusing it.

The electricity went out today and gave us a taste of hell. The ceiling fans stopped, and the electric stove wouldn't work, so there was no cooking, no food, and not even a cup of tea to be had. The electric water pump also stopped, so there was no water in the taps. Since some of our cellmates are elderly and unwell, we banned smoking, because there's less oxygen to go around when the fans aren't working. Three of them, who have heart problems, spent the day sitting by the door just to get a breath of air, and one young man took his towel and stood there whirling it in circles around his head to imitate a fan for them.

Finished Rabee Jaber's *The Blue Butterfly*. Can't help wondering why he never wrote a Lebanese version of the Egyptian soap

Hilmiyya Nights, or moved to Mexico to make a career writing telenovelas.

The prisoners here constantly copy and imitate one another. It starts with in-jokes and catchphrases, but they also do it with the way they talk and how they pronounce their letters. Even the English that some of our foreign cellmates speak gets twisted; odd words show up in the pidgin taking shape inside the cellblock, and Arabic words and letters find their way into their English sentences too. In a closed environment like this, language seems to spread like a virus, its DNA adapting and reconfiguring itself with each interaction.

POWER'S PEACE OF MIND

THE HIGHEST AUTHORITIES IN THE prison were the warden and the chief of intelligence, followed by the descending ranks of the police. Any request or issue bearing any relation to me had to go through the chief of intelligence, a man called Muhammad, whom his men referred to as the Bey—or, the way they said it, "Mahamma Beh."

Convicted prisoners weren't allowed visits in their first thirty days—for pretrial detainees, eleven—but these rules could be sidestepped with permission from the public prosecutor's office. I got my first visit, from my lawyer Mahmoud Othman, a few days in. As we sat on the visitors' bench surrounded by three plainclothes men, Mahmoud told me he'd brought some books and letters from Yasmine and my friends. After the visit, I inquired about the books and letters and was told they were with Mahamma Beh. He had to inspect them first.

I squirmed impatiently for three days straight, lying on my bunk and pacing the cellblock. Whenever any of the security officers walked by or came in to help themselves to some of the pasta we'd cooked—the guards often took our food—I would hand them a pack of cigarettes and ask about the books and letters. When I urged them to pass my question on to Mahamma Beh, they blew me off with excuses like "He's left for the day," or "He's busy; his door's closed," but promised to mention it to him next time they saw him. Finally, on the fourth day, I was given one letter and two of the books.

It took me a long time to figure out how to get things done in prison. I observed the occasional changes of leadership, followed the rise and fall of individual officers through the ranks, listened to the gossip of the older prisoners, and paid attention to what the guards bitched about when you gave them cigarettes or fruit. Through these Barthesian fragments of knowledge, I came to understand that the primary function of any power—including our own Mahamma Beh—is to widen its own sphere of influence through perpetual conflict and the swift elimination of peers and superiors. The secondary function is peace of mind. Power doesn't like disruption, or any kind of annoyance coming from the direction of the people it controls; it has enough to deal with in the shape of its competitors and those above it in the hierarchy. I realized my insistent requests about Mahmoud's delivery were just a source of annoyance to those on the lowest rungs of power.

I didn't get the books and letters until much later. The security guys lied to me; mostly, they never passed on my requests to Mahamma Beh. They didn't want to annoy him: to cause annoyance would be to fail in their task of faithfully guarding power's peace of mind. They were just sheepdogs. Jail dogs. They exploited my position of need to extract more cigarettes and fruit, like heathen priests consuming the offerings I brought without ever delivering my supplications to their stone god.

Day 4: Wednesday, February 24, 2016

Cellblock 2/4, Tura Agricultural Prison. To mark the passage of time, and retain some memory of the days as they go by, I have to write things down. Keeping a diary is a survival mechanism. It stops me from being swept away in the current that is the peculiar rhythm—so different from time on the outside—of prison life.

A prison year, with time off for good behavior, is approximately eight months, or two-thirds of the sentence. Compressing the months of the year has some kind of cumulative effect on the weeks, the days, and even the hours. I don't know if I'm imagining things or if time really is up to something, but I spent the last night staring at the tiny hands of the clock on the wall moving in the darkness. I was so convinced that the second hand was ticking more slowly than it did outside prison that I actually asked a sleepless cellmate about it. He stared at the clock with me for a few moments, then said doubtfully, "Maybe the battery's going."

I noticed one guy has a drooping bunch of red roses in the window next to him. So maybe we could get mint and basil, plant them in plastic bottles to liven the place up a bit and make it smell nicer. Maybe I could even get jasmine for Yasmine.

LOVE IN THE
VISITING ROOM

IN THE VISITING ROOM, WHERE prisoners and their families sat on concrete benches with the ants and cockroaches, I saw the toughest men I'd ever met break down in tears on their mothers', wives', or girlfriends' bosoms. These slipups just happened sometimes, despite your best efforts to stay in control. You knew that showing weakness or grief in front of your family wouldn't do any good; all it would do was make them worry more.

Before your first visit, a more experienced cellmate would tell you to shave and comb your hair nicely. Someone would lend you some hair gel, someone else would let you have a spritz of the cologne they kept in a plastic bottle, and a third would offer you a piece of advice: "Make sure you're looking as nice as possible in front of your family. Otherwise, they'll worry about you, or get even more upset than they are already, especially after getting up so early and coming all the way here and waiting for hours in the baking heat before being allowed in."

Whenever a visit approached, certain rituals had to be performed: "ironing" your clothes by laying them out underneath the mattress, getting a haircut from the prison barber in exchange for a pack of cigarettes, waking up early to shower and shave—it was like getting ready for a date. And at the end of the day, that's what it was: these were the few minutes of romance that you were allowed, and by applying yourself diligently as you prepared for each visit, you were nourishing that romance to make sure it survived.

When men are thrown into prison, their friends and social circles suddenly vanish, and the only people left are their mothers, wives, or girlfriends. They are the ones who stay in touch, who visit faithfully, who prepare homemade food, and who offer a snatched embrace at the beginning and end of each visit.

Shortly after I received my second visit, the chief of intelligence summoned me to his office and told me that my fiancée had inquired about the procedures for getting married in prison. Yasmine and I weren't actually engaged; we'd met just nine months previously, at a music festival in South Sinai. We had been practically living together, but Egyptian law recognized official contracts, not relationships of love, and so Yasmine made sure to introduce herself to the prison authorities as my fiancée; it didn't technically qualify her for visiting rights, but the officials were indulgent with us.

Yasmine was also a prominent human rights lawyer. When we met, I already had two lawyers, and she thought it wouldn't be professional to get involved. So she sat next to me in the trial, and when I was sentenced, she used her attorney's privileges to visit me and to assist with my case. But lawyers needed official permission each time they visited the prison, so marriage seemed like the logical next move for us.

The chief of intelligence had told her what was required, but wanted to check that I consented so it wouldn't look like he'd set me up. He gave a sleazy smile. I got the impression that he, along with the other officers, was enjoying my romance with Yasmine, and that's why they were temporarily bending the rules by letting her visit as a "relative"; the possibility that Their Excellencies might one day change their minds was a source of anxiety to us both. If we were married, Yasmine would officially be allowed to visit me, regardless of the chief of intelligence and his whims. But it scared us. We knew that no matter how long my sentence seemed to last, I was in prison only temporarily, and we didn't want the memories of our wedding day to consist of the hideous smiles of the prison guards and me in a roach-infested blue uniform and handcuffs.

Following the demonstrations in April 2016 against Egypt's transfer of Tiran and Sanafir Islands to Saudi Arabia, a bunch of the young protesters who'd been detained were brought to the prison I was in. The atmosphere was tense, and the guards were testy. I went down to the visiting room at my allotted time to find only my mother there, with no sign of my brother or Yasmine. Panicking, a thousand scenarios went through my head: What could possibly have happened to them? A few seconds later my brother appeared from the office of the chief of intelligence. "They're not letting Yasmine in," he said.

The families of the new prisoners were waiting at the prison gate, and the administration had decided not to recognize the visitor permits they carried. Being a lawyer, Yasmine had tried to intervene on behalf of the families and pressure the administration to let the visits go ahead, and they'd gotten pissed off and decided not to let her in either.

The chief of intelligence called me into his office and delivered a lengthy monologue about how he'd broken regulations out of sheer indulgence and sympathy, and would personally prefer to let Yasmine visit me. But if she was going to cause trouble and get involved in matters that didn't concern her, then he'd have to do things by the book. I stood sullenly in front of him. It was the nastiest power game you could think of, and they were playing me as they'd played so many thousands of other activists, political figures, and ordinary Egyptians. He knew that if he spoke to Yasmine herself, she'd be adamant about the provisions of the law, her prerogatives as a lawyer, and the families' right to visit their detained children; but if he spoke to me from his position of power, jailer to prisoner, then I'd talk to Yasmine myself, conveying the same message in the form of emotional pressure, and that would extract exactly the concessions he was after.

I felt utterly helpless, and with that came the peace of indifference. I raised my head and for the first time confronted him directly. "I don't care," I said. "I want to see Yasmine this visit."

He let her come in for a few minutes at the end of the visit that day. Without words, over the course of a few weeks, the chief of intelligence and I came to a tacit agreement. He'd realized that all I cared about was books, Yasmine, and the letters we wrote to each other (which everybody employed in the prison creepily passed around before they were delivered, and that was after they'd undergone multiple inspections and spent days being shown to all the different security services). So he hung on to those three things, knowing he could get me to do what he wanted by dangling them as carrots or using them as sticks. Every time he let me take one of the books that had arrived for me, he'd quip, "Go on, then. Take your piece of opium."

The visiting room was the place where emotions were set loose: tears, laughter, the strained elation that expressed all the other feelings that hadn't been able to take their usual form. All this had to happen under the eyes of the guards and the other prisoners. Things were especially difficult for the women visitors who happened to wear the full face veil. One of our cellmates confessed in a moment of weakness that he hadn't seen his wife's face for eighteen months; for him, visits were simply an extension of his imprisonment. In the visiting room, as in his cell, he had to conjure his wife's features from memory.

Another attempted to get around the visiting room regulations by having his sister stand holding a prayer rug in front him and his wife, so his wife could lift her face veil without the rest of the room seeing. The guards turned a blind eye to the makeshift curtain at first, but before long, one of them cleared his throat and said, "That's not allowed." The sister rolled up the prayer mat, the wife lowered her face veil, and the brief moment of privacy they'd managed to create for themselves evaporated.

The prison regulations stipulated a full hour for visits, but it was rare to ever get that full hour. Visiting began whenever the lieutenant on duty felt like it, and when he rang the bell it was time for goodbyes and embraces. The birdies got extra visit time in exchange for the information they provided about their cellmates; so did those lucky inmates who happened to have friends in high places. As the chief of intelligence would say, they got one little piece of opium more than everybody else.

Day 11: Wednesday, March 2, 2016

Dreams are an opening through which I'm visited by things I miss. I repeatedly dream of the sea, the beach, food, friends, and lovers.

I've tried controlling what I dream about using what I know about sleep science and mind-training techniques. For example, I'll spend the whole day focusing on a specific person I miss, and later those thoughts will follow me into sleep, and that person, or something related to them, will show up in my dream. Sometimes it doesn't work, though, so I've come up with another strategy that involves avoiding thinking about that person. Whenever my mind turns to them, I quickly think about something else, until finally I'm asleep and the repressed memory of that person imposes itself on the world of my dreams.

I also follow Henry Miller's advice and record my dreams. My black notebook and a pen live right next to my bunk, and the first thing I do when I wake up is write down everything I dreamed about. You have to do this while you're still half-asleep, held captive in the world of your dreams. If you wash your face or drink water first, you'll be recording your memories of the dream as an outsider to the world of sleep. The dimensions and measurements don't look like they do in the mirror.

Once my dream is written down, I spend the day squeezing every last drop from the memory of it: the taste of sweets, the laughter of my friends, spectral erotic encounters, and erections brought on by desire and love instead of by miserable, bored masturbation.

TRUTH IS A MANGO

I CAN'T THINK OF ANY literary genre that lies as habitually about its subject, or is as artistically lazy while claiming authenticity, as prison literature.

Prison literature presents itself as offering up a truth that the ordinary reader could never otherwise obtain. The prison writer demands humility and deference from their reader. *I have been through hell*, declares the writer. *I have no reason to lie. I simply record. I write out of loyalty to my cellmates and everything we went through together.* And since the prison experience is so noble, so venerated, the writer doesn't see why they should be bound by considerations of craft or aesthetics. Some even argue that to aestheticize prison in one's writing is a dereliction of the duty to reveal the truth, and that the beauty of the text lies in its honesty and authenticity. There's a saying in Arabic, "Al-sidq mangah": "The truth is a refuge." Or, as one of my cellmates pronounced it in colloquial fashion: "Al-sidq manga": "Truth's a mango."

Egypt's experiments in prison literature are full of contradictions. In the 1960s, Gamal Abdel Nasser's prisons were home to both Islamists and communists, and members of the two movements recorded their experiences so differently that you start to wonder how truthful they were; it sometimes feels like they were deliberately attempting to frustrate any understanding of what prison was like at the time. But their dissimilarity is a reflection of their individuality rather than their honesty. There can be no universally acknowledged truth when each prisoner goes through such a different experience and feels such a personal pain.

Truth demands consensus and proof. But prison writings rely on personal narrative alone. Any untruth or inconsistency can be explained away as the work of prison itself, and when the story doesn't make sense or its plausibility is called into question, the writer-narrator still has honesty on their side. Contradiction and error can't be helped when prison puts people under such extreme pressure.

Then there's the dead weight of ideology that drags on these writings. Prison literature has always played a part in political conflict in the same way that prison itself, in the mind of the political prisoner, is an unavoidable feature of the political struggle. Most Arabic prison literature I've read has been produced by political prisoners for whom writing is just an extension of their activism. It stops them from going crazy, or keeps their soul from dying, while they wait for the better future they're going to build with their party or organization when they get out. Or, if they're writing after the fact, then they do so to inscribe the experiences of their movement on the walls of history, to make a scratch— however small—on the towering facade of power and the narrative it imposes. So the artistry of whatever's written about isn't what matters to the imprisoned activist writer; the important thing is the documentary content of the text and what it can do to serve the literary-political cause.

But documents and testimonies aren't literature and are certainly not art. And if art has documentary value, it is only secondary. A document attempts to explain, to educate the public. Literature exists unto itself; its essence lies in its singularity, not in its expository abilities. And it's from works of literature that writers learn their craft. In a work of literature, form is central; indeed, form and content are one—that's what makes the work. In documents and testimonies of imprisonment, content dominates, and form is just a means to an end.

A political prisoner is never on their own in prison, even if they were arrested and interrogated alone. In the writings of political prisoners, there's always the moment when the writer meets their comrades on the inside. There's always a clear distinction drawn between political and criminal imprisonment too. Political writers like to make it clear that they're different from the criminal prisoners, even when they share a cell.

Prison, for these writers, is a crucible in which the political collective is forged, its members' commitments are put to the test, and the bonds between them are strengthened. Only the symbolism varies: with the Islamists, tears flow as they bow and kneel together for the dawn prayer; with the communists, members quiver and burst into flaming orgasm when their comrades' voices join in a Shaykh Imam song.

In the end, the prison writings I've read aren't really about prison. They're extended analyses of the political moment in which they were written, with prison just another arena in which political conflict plays out. It's an arena that sees the writer defeated yet defiant—but nobody prepared me for that moment, and nobody told me what the experience would be like. I always expected I'd end up in prison, like anyone involved in public life in Egypt, but I never imagined it would be art—literature, a novel—that would put me there. I ended up in prison as a writer, not as a political activist.

Day 21: Saturday, March 12, 2016

Most of my cellmates are inordinately interested in their dreams. It's the main topic of conversation. People tell their dreams to trusted confidants, hoping for an interpretation. Or someone will shout to a cellmate that they've seen a blessed vision of them in their dream.

Dreams are a glimpse of hope, a window onto the outside world. At least, that's what they say in Europe and advanced places like that. But in Egyptian prisons—built by our British colonizers—dreams take on far more complex dimensions that overlap and intermingle with a core of religious faith. "Surat

Yusuf," the story of Joseph, is the prisoner's constant companion, and most prisoners' favorite surah in the whole Qur'an.

Injustice and imprisonment are the basic subjects of the story.
Yusuf, the victim of a conspiracy by his brothers, is exiled to
Egypt. There he falls victim to another conspiracy, and is thrown
into prison because his beauty and chastity drive the women
of Egypt wild. In prison, he and his cellmates have no window
from which to look out onto the world, save their dreams. Two
cellmates dream, and Yusuf interprets: one will die, and another
will earn great favor with the king.

Because he is a prophet, Yusuf's interpretation proves
correct. The cellmate who survives becomes an adviser to the
king. Sometime later, the king has an obscure recurring dream,
and the adviser remembers Yusuf, his old cellmate, and coun-
sels the king to have him released from prison. Yusuf is freed
and is himself made adviser to the king, and chancellor of all of
Egypt's treasury. Now in a position of power, he is able to strike
back against his brothers and avenge himself of everything he
has lost in life.

The story has inspired prisoners across the world and
throughout the ages. They see themselves in Yusuf—wronged
like he was—or imagine themselves as Yusuf's companions.
Prisoners fall asleep fervently hoping for a vision that will bring
good tidings.

Here in prison, dreams aren't a confused muddle; they're
the very core of one's convictions. We go to our bunks at night
expecting visions, waiting to find out what will happen, and

anxiously hoping the news will be good. Our greatest wish is to dream we are cupbearers to the king; our greatest fear is to dream we are crucified, and that birds are pecking at our heads.

EARLY LESSONS IN BURNING BOOKS

MY FAMILY HAS A RECORD when it comes to getting rid of books.

When I was very young and we lived in Egypt, we had a ritual that took place at regular intervals. My father would throw open the cupboards and drawers and make an inventory of all the books, magazines, and notebooks stored inside, a task that could take hours. The most important items were the journals containing his notes on the books he'd read; next came his collection of books by Islamist leaders such as Sayyid Qutb and Hassan al-Banna.

First my father would sort the books into groups, then distribute them among a number of hiding places. Some would be stored in cardboard boxes on the roof next to the chicken coop; others would be left for safekeeping with neighbors who weren't involved in any political activism. Finally, he would decide that some books were too dangerous to keep—dangerous for him and for us. He could always get hold of another copy of them if he really needed to, and so he would burn them and painstakingly dispose of their ashes.

I didn't pay much attention to this habit of his as a child; I thought everybody burned the books they didn't want. My mom struggled to explain the delicate political situation to her young child, so instead she would say, "Those books contain writings from the Qur'an—God's words—so it's not right to put them out with the trash."

My grandfather, who worked as a guard at a factory, had an enormous library. At one point, according to my father, he was so poor he couldn't even afford a bed, so he stacked up his volumes of astronomy and the collected poetry of Ahmad Shawqi (which, in any case, he knew by heart) for his children to sleep on. For reasons too complicated to go into, he fell into a deep depression in the early '80s and got rid of almost his entire collection; after that, he made do with reading the news-paper—*al-Akhbar*, to be precise—or dipping into the poetry of al-Ma'arri. He also held on to some of his beloved astronomy books. He loved astronomy so much that he named his first son Galileo, and when people protested that Galileo wasn't a Muslim name, he changed it reluctantly to Naji, but had the front of the house emblazoned with the name NAJI GALILEO in large calligraphic script.

Unlike my grandfather's book burning, my father's wasn't the result of a sudden depression, or even a decline in his ability to read. Instead, it was spurred by the possibility that his books could be used as evidence against him if the house was raided or he was arrested. My father was a member of the Muslim Brotherhood, and the orders to burn books in fact came from senior figures in the organization, who were keen to keep their members out of trouble. A single copy of Hassan al-Banna's *Letters* or *A Movement Approach to the Prophetic Biography* was enough to indict a person for membership in a banned organization.

And so, on dull summer evenings, when we were home from Kuwait and spending time in al-Mansura, there wasn't much to do apart from sitting around and reading the works of Anis Mansur and Khalid Muhammad Khalid, or the plays of Tawfiq al-Hakim. Those were the kinds of books my father deemed safe enough to be found if State Security ever raided our home. And I didn't need to read al-Banna's books to find out about the Brotherhood, because the Brotherhood were just a part of my life.

In Kuwait, as in Egypt and numerous other countries, the Brotherhood form a vast social welfare network that supports not only individual members, but their families too. Not a week went by without me attending some joint activity with the children of other Brotherhood families residing in Kuwait. As well as reading the Qur'an and learning about the life of the Prophet, we were taken on weekend trips. For a child like me, who'd moved very abruptly to Kuwait from al-Mansura, these days out with the Brotherhood Cubs provided a warm and welcoming environment that promised new discoveries and the chance to make friends.

Things were a bit different when we moved back to Egypt. The Muslim Brotherhood had become a banned organization, and even mentioning the name in front of the wrong people could land you in prison. They existed as a sort of public secret, and their events and activities were held more discreetly than they had been in Kuwait. I got a lot of attention in our village because my father occupied a prominent position within the organization; he was a doctor, and someone the Cubs looked up to, although I didn't realize that at the time. I was always reminded of how much people respected him when I met a brother for the first time. "You're Naji Higazi's son!" they'd exclaim. "Praise the Lord, that's wonderful."

Day 52: Tuesday, April 12, 2016

Dreamed I was let out of prison for a day. I went to see my mom in a house that wasn't our home, and found her standing on a balcony high above the street, hanging out the laundry. I stood beside her in silence, then she pointed to a flight of stairs leading to the roof and led me up them and out of the house. At the top I suddenly found myself running down a road: I knew I had to get to the airport because my dad and siblings were on an airplane waiting for me, but I quickly got lost in the unfamiliar city streets. I got tired of running and walking, so I stopped in a narrow street similar to the alleyways of Old Cairo. I came across a boy; he was selling hash, and when he saw me looking exhausted and hungry, he handed me some bread with a piece of hash inside it and told me to eat.

The bread was fresh and warm and delicious. As I took bites out of it from one side, smoke puffed out of the other side, as if the hash were burning inside the bread. The boy struck up a conversation, and some friends of his appeared.

Suddenly a police patrol was attacking us. The boy set off at a sprint and I ran after him through the labyrinthine alleyways, but he quickly disappeared and I was lost. Finally, I came to a dead end. I turned to retrace my steps, but the street in front of me was a dead end too. On either side were closed doors and windows. I ran back and forth from one dead end of the street to the other, terrified the police would arrest me, and pushed in desperation at one of the doors, only to find myself in another alleyway identical to the first—or perhaps it was the same one.

A MODERN ISLAMIC UPBRINGING

FOR MOST OF MY CHILDHOOD, both in Kuwait and after our return to Egypt, I attended private schools whose names included the words *modern languages* and *Islamic*. Language schools are a prestigious kind of school in Egypt, and these two catchphrases summed up the particular combination of tradition and modernity that Mom and Dad decided should be the foundation of my upbringing. There are three main elements in Egyptian private schools: clean toilets, religion classes, and advanced English courses.

Guidance and Light Islamic School of Modern Languages, where I spent my third year of middle school after we moved back from Kuwait, was a well-known Brotherhood school. My father had in fact helped set it up, under the aegis of the Brotherhood's School and Educational Services section, an area of activity that the organization had greatly expanded since the 1980s, both as an economic investment and as an effective method of grassroots proselytizing. We followed the same curriculum as state-run schools, but we took an additional two classes per week: one on a subject called "Holy Qur'an" and another that was a mixture of the life stories of major religious figures and Islamic lifestyle tips. Instead of music classes, we studied "Islamic Hymns." Musical instruments were banned, with the exception of some basic percussion instruments like the tabl and daff. The school walls were covered with posters and wall newspapers detailing the dangers of listening to instrumental music. The Islamic hymns we were obliged to memorize, meanwhile, were a greatest hits of repurposed nationalist songs and anthems, with the word *Islam* substituted wherever the word *Egypt* appeared.

The school's pupils included the sons of all the local Brotherhood leadership, along with other Muslim boys from an assortment of different socioeconomic backgrounds. It's only now that I realize I never even met a Christian until I was fourteen; I lived in a parallel universe with its own moral code and cosmic vision, its own definition of a virtuous life, and its own guiding mission.

Leaving the warm womb of the Brotherhood school system for Taha Hussein Public Secondary was like crossing an ocean or traveling through space to another planet. Sending me there was a financial decision, but also a sign they thought I was old enough to be thrown into real life. For the first time, I had Christian classmates, and access to a library containing more than just prayer books. It was stuffed with volumes that had been gathering dust since the '60s. The rosy world I'd been accustomed to—where brothers walked around smiling genially, clutching toothbrush twigs in imitation of the Prophet, and nobody ever used curse words—began to seem suffocating and isolated.

Against the background of the Second Palestinian Intifada, I was propelled up through the Brotherhood ranks, and even though I was still only in high school, I spent my time with brothers who were already at university. I helped write the chants that we would shout at the huge demonstrations that took place after the killing of twelve-year-old Muhammad al-Durrah in Gaza. I was an active member of the al-Azhar University chapter of the Muslim Brotherhood. And then the Haydar Haydar thing happened.

REFUSING A SEAT
AT THE BANQUET

ONE DAY A BROTHER SHOWED up carrying a copy of the newspaper the *People*. He put it down on the chair next to him and our meeting got underway in its usual fashion. We began with Qur'an recitations, then a brother explained a prophetic hadith, and then another read from Muhammad al-Ghazali's *Jurisprudence of the Prophetic Biography*. Finally, the brother with the newspaper opened it and began to read an item out loud.

The news was about the republication of a novel by the Syrian writer Haydar Haydar by the Egyptian Ministry of Culture. This novel, *A Banquet for Seaweed*, not only contained depictions of sex, but insulted God and the Prophet Muhammad, peace be upon him. We had to respond—and that meant protests and calls for the book to be burned.

"The book must be burned," repeated the brother earnestly. Without even thinking about it, I objected. I was the poet of the group—an Islamic poet, of course—and I said I wasn't going to write slogans calling for that book, or any other, to be burned.

I still have no idea why I picked that particular hill to die on. But a couple of days later, while I was leafing through my grandfather's copy of *al-Akhbar*, searching for material to support my position, I saw an advertisement for *Literature Review* (or in its Arabic title, *Akhbar al-Adab*). It showed the cover of the current issue and listed the features, almost all of which focused on the Haydar Haydar case, arguing for freedom of expression and defending the novel's publishers. This stance was at odds with the position of *al-Akhbar*, the parent newspaper, whose managing board and editor in chief, Ibrahim Sa'da, were opposed to the novel. I couldn't get hold of *Literature Review* in any of the places I usually hung out, so I asked a university student friend to buy me a copy. The moment I opened the magazine, I knew I had stepped through a door into another world, and that there would be no going back.

At meetings I remained staunchly opposed to calls for the book to be confiscated and burned, and I refused to participate in any protests against Haydar's novel. The Brotherhood were pouring oil on the flames. The student chapter organized demonstrations and released statement after incendiary statement, taking advantage of the controversy to drum up support for the upcoming elections. At the time, I wasn't fully aware of the complex political dimensions of the situation. I was just a teenager and I was still working out who I was, but certain values and principles were starting to become important to me, and I clung to them in my attempts to impose some idealism on the outside world.

In one of our weekly meetings, a brother read out several passages from the novel, which had been excerpted in the *People*. I didn't even like what I heard, but that was no justification, in my view, for burning the book. I got embroiled in a long discussion with the brothers, voices were raised, and the brother in charge began remonstrating angrily that I was thinking dangerous thoughts. I argued back, and finally he shouted, "Either you give up those books you read and these ideas you've been having, or you stop showing up here."

I turned and left, and I never went back.

Day 13: Friday, March 4, 2016

The circle has closed. The outside world is receding. The tiny spark of hope that I would be out of here soon has been extinguished. Any talk of an objection or appeal is pure fantasy. I might as well spit in my hand and get my cock wet, ready for a long, slow fuck with despair.

SHAMBARA

SHARP METAL OBJECTS OF ANY KIND were banned in prison, and this ban gave rise to numerous ingenious ways of repurposing anything that could be salvaged or snuck in. I was always intrigued by the names that were given to these upcycled tools. For example, if you carefully removed the top of a tin of beans or tuna, cleaned it, and flattened it, its sharp edges could be used as a knife for chopping vegetables or peeling fruit, which was known as a "shambara." The verb was "to shambar," so you'd be told to "shambar the tomatoes for the salad"; or, by way of threat, someone might say, "I swear to god I'll shambar you!"

Words like these had no place outside prison; this way of talking had no life other than between these four walls. The language was imprisoned with us. It was a companion with whom we shared our cell.

Day 79: Monday, May 9, 2016

Dreamed I was the victim of some kind of marriage I'd gotten myself into. Suddenly I was the husband of an ignorant, superficial, vacuous wife, whose family were awful parasites. We lived in a place that was supposedly our house, and my friend Wael Abd El-Fattah was visiting us at the same time as my in-laws, one of whom looked just like one of my cellmates. They were causing chaos and being a pain in every corner of the house, and in the end, the only place Wael and I could find to talk was the bathroom. We locked the door behind us, knowing that outside they were stealing the radio and the TV and all the electrical appliances. The issue didn't bother me in the least. The issue was how I was going to get rid of them.

Day 80: Tuesday, May 10, 2016

Dreamed I was in the flat of D, one of my cellmates, getting ready for a New Year's Eve party. The guests started arriving, but they were wearing masks. Everyone was getting into the party mood except me, and I spent most of the time worrying that the security services would raid us and hoping everyone would just leave and get home safely so I could go home too.

That's twice now that I've dreamed about someone from my cellblock. Is it a sign that the old world's receding? Is this my world now? Have the prison walls penetrated so deeply into my unconscious that they're now controlling my dreams too? Am I losing my only window onto the outside? Will despair consolidate its power now that the blockade is complete? If I surrender now and kill what hope remains, will it give me some relief and help me adapt more quickly to my new home?

THAT SMELL AND
OTHER STORIES

BOOKS WOULD APPEAR AND DISAPPEAR. The library lent out
books daily to prisoners spread across nine cellblocks, and sometimes they'd be gone for weeks at a time before reappearing—on
their own shelf or somewhere else entirely. I used to scan the
shelves repeatedly, making a mental note of which books had
vanished or resurfaced overnight.

One day my gaze fell on a slim book of no more than 150
pages. It was black, with a title in a splashy red font: *That Smell
and Other Stories* by Sonallah Ibrahim. I laughed out loud when
I saw it, disturbing the elderly men who spent their time in
the quiet library. Still surprised and amused at the coincidence,
I got a grip on myself, borrowed the book, and went back
downstairs to my cell. I waited till lights-out to turn on the
homemade lamp I'd bought off another prisoner for two packs of
Cleopatra cigarettes and lay back on my bunk to start the book.

The inside cover bore the official stamp of the Ministry of the Interior. This was a book that had been banned in the 1960s, yet now, in the 2010s, it was not only permitted but was being distributed by the Prisons Authority itself, in its own libraries.

Within the first few pages, I discovered that the edition of the book I'd read previously was an abridged version. The copy I held in my hands had been published in 1983 by Mustaqbal, based in Cairo and Alexandria, and surprisingly carried no Egyptian National Library deposit number; as well as the novella and three short stories, it included a long introduction by Ibrahim himself, a foreword by Yusuf Idris that had been written in the '60s but never published, and the much older writer Yahya Haqqi's infamous article denouncing the book for its explicit language and depictions of vulgar physicality.

In his introduction, Ibrahim recounts how he wrote the novella after spending years in the Oases Prison, an infamously harsh facility located deep in the Western Desert. Imprisoned originally for his political activities, he came out with a strengthened conviction about the necessity of literature and art. He also discusses the playwright and novelist Kamal al-Qilish and the writer Ra'uf Mus'ad's manifesto-like introduction, written for the book's original publication. The text affirms literature's power to penetrate to the truth of existence, and calls upon literature and the arts to fight colonialism by exposing and challenging bourgeois values—the mission of any truly revolutionary art. (In interviews many years later, Ibrahim would say that the sole purpose of literature is pleasure. Al-Qilish died in 2004, and Mus'ad is still alive and well, chasing the ghosts of his desires and fighting virtual battles on Facebook. As far as I'm concerned, whether your aim is to end imperialism and destroy bourgeois respectability, or simply to bring pleasure, it's unlikely that anyone but you will remember why you wrote what you did.)

Idris loved the book, and as an official literary star, he used his foreword to heap praise on the skinny young writer and his explosive talent. But the publishing industry was run by the state at the time, and all printed matter was subject to censorship; neither al-Qilish and Mus'ad's revolutionary communiqué nor Idris's approving foreword did anything to help Ibrahim's case, and the censors refused to allow the book to be published. This caused such an uproar in intellectual circles that the minister of culture, a former military man named 'Abd al-Qadir Hatim—who, in Nasser's military state, had final authority over literary matters—became personally involved.

Ibrahim was summoned to the minister's office, where Hatim and his assistants immediately began to banter and joke among themselves, ridiculing the novella and its author. Hatim questioned Ibrahim about one scene in particular that had caught his attention, in which the protagonist tries unsuccessfully to have sex with a prostitute that his friends have picked up for him. "What's the problem?" asked the concerned minister. "Can't he get it up?" He and his assistants exploded in laughter all over again in appreciation of His Excellency's clever sense of humor.

So the novella didn't make it past the censors in Cairo, and the edition I'd read long before I went to prison was printed in Beirut, where, as Ibrahim explains in his introduction, the interfering publisher had censored offending words and phrases. The first unabridged edition was the one I was holding in my hands.

Commenting on the charge of violating public decency that Hatim's spies had pinned on him, Ibrahim asks: "Why is it demanded of us… that we write about creatures whose orifices are virtually non-existent so as not to offend the fabricated decency of readers who know more about sex than the author himself does?"

CROSS-EXAMINATION

What do you have to say regarding the text titled "An Extract from Using Life," in which the journalist Ahmed Naji employs language grossly offensive to public decency, namely in his complete depiction of a sexual encounter with a female friend named "Spoon," which starts with his fondling of her knee and ends with his removal of a condom after they have performed intercourse?

—From the public prosecution's cross-examination of Tarek al-Taher, editor in chief of *Literature Review*

NIPPLES AND POINTS

SONALLAH IBRAHIM WAS A POLITICAL PRISONER. Only after he'd been to prison was his novel banned for offending public morality. Ibrahim was in prison alongside his comrades, his teachers, and his fellow Communist Party members. They talked; they consoled one another; they forged bonds of friendship and brotherhood in prison. Together they fomented revolution in literature and the arts. Ibrahim had people to share his ideas with, including Mus'ad and al-Qilish.

I was in prison for moral crimes. My book never got banned or confiscated, and my conviction rested on a single chapter that happened to be republished in *Literature Review*. In prison I found myself in a cellblock with the Beys. These high-class prisoners were mostly former state employees—judges of varying seniority, high-ranking police officers, or military men— who were in for drugs or corruption offenses. They read to pass the time, and they were desperate to tell you about what they were reading, seemingly with the sole aim of exhibiting their own limited intelligence.

One time I was sitting alone when a former army officer convicted of running a car theft ring called out loudly, in front of the whole cellblock, "Mr. Naji! Seeing as you spend all day reading, do you know what 'Antara ibn Shaddad's mother was called?"

I said nothing, but looked up from the Eduardo Galeano book in my hand to find five more of our cellmates watching in anticipation. The man himself was a slimy piece of work who relayed every single letter uttered in the cellblock to the chief of intelligence, and at this point I was still new, so I didn't want any trouble on top of the shit I was already in. I shrugged—why the hell would I know what a sixth-century poet's mom was called?—and gave a polite schoolboy's answer.

"No, no idea."

"Come on!" he scoffed. "That's an easy one. Honestly. A writer, and he doesn't know the name of 'Antara ibn Shaddad's mother!"

He liked people to call him "General," so I replied, "I don't know, General. Maybe she's just known as Mother of 'Antara."

The assembled men laughed, and he guffawed obnoxiously. "Nope."

"So what is it?" I said. "At least you can teach me something new."

He snickered even more obnoxiously than before and said, "I'm not telling." Then he turned and went back to his bunk.

Ibrahim discussed Hemingway with his cellmates! And
Soviet poetry! The best I got was this. Or conversations about
Ahmed Mourad thrillers and Mohamed Sadek psychodramas.
Or horror literature. On rare occasions, some of my cellmates
had read some of Ibrahim or Khairy Shalaby's work. One time,
a guy came over to talk to me about Ibrahim's *That Smell*, which
he'd just finished.

"This has nipples in it!" he said, waving the book at me.
"Isn't that a violation of public decency too?!"

I smiled and said that Ibrahim had used the words *the two
points of her breasts* rather than *nipples*. And in any case, he didn't
need to worry, because the book had been banned back in the
day. Apparently "points" were once enough to offend; now they
were permitted even in prison libraries.

Day 87: Tuesday, May 17, 2016

Prison creates a sense of solidarity that works in strange ways
and is never conditional upon your situation or the nature of
your case. Here's one example. Uncle S is charged with some
small-scale fraud offense. It's not his first time; in fact, he's a
professional who boasts that he will get straight back to work as
soon as he's out. Obviously, I like him, because he's honest and
doesn't feign innocence like the rest mostly do. More crucially,
he's funny, a skillful teller of jokes that offend public decency.

Today, Uncle S was granted release with bail set at one thousand Egyptian pounds, a sum he doesn't have. But within two
hours, the cellblock had come up with the money. Everyone

donated however many cigarettes they could, and before long we had eighty packs, which at the prison exchange rate meant approximately twelve hundred pounds. These were sent to the nabatshi to be exchanged for cash, which was then transferred to Miss H, one of the civilian administrators, who, in exchange for a tip, helps prisoners get tasks done on the outside. She paid the bail at the public prosecution cashier's office, and Uncle S was out by the end of the day.

PLEASING MYSELF

I'VE NEVER FELT MUCH INCLINATION to revolt against imperialism in its liberal capitalist form. That was what Sonallah Ibrahim and his generation cared about, the cause that pushed them to search for a truly revolutionary literature. Ibrahim spent his literary career constructing complex, harmonious architectures of fiction that demonstrated, over and over again, that capitalism was evil and that multinational corporations had ascended to the rapacious throne vacated by pre–World War II colonialism. But toward the end of his life, he announced frankly and clearly in a newspaper interview that "what really matters is aesthetic pleasure."

Do writers write for the sake of other people's pleasure? If they do, which might appear to be the case on the surface, then what about their own? Writers are criticized, analyzed, interpreted, even thrown into prison on account of their pleasure, and yet their pleasure is by no means a satisfactory justification, from the point of view of society and its various institutions, for what they do. Instead, it cloaks itself in more noble guises: intellectual edification, revolutionary commitment, self-expression, dialogue.

As far as I'm concerned, these pretexts are just scattershot attempts by writers to distract attention from their central motive, which is their own satisfaction. Yet this idea remains taboo, illegitimate. Writers don't get to demand that society respect their right to unadulterated pleasure and joy, so instead they enumerate literature's virtues, its contribution to civilization, its historical value. It's like a person claiming they have sex because they want to help ensure the survival of the human race.

On the journey that began when I was first remanded, then taken in a police van from court to precinct and from precinct to prison, I met prisoners charged with all sorts of criminal and political offenses, plainclothes informers, lowly police cadets, and officers all the way up to the general who reported to the minister of the interior himself. They all wanted to know what my "story" was, and how and why it had gotten me sentenced to two years in prison.

I would automatically start explaining the broad plotlines of the book: an earthquake hits Cairo in sandstorm season and the city disappears under rubble and dust. At this point, the police officers would interrupt and ask, "Yeah, but did you offend someone, or what?"

"No," I'd say. "It was a novel. There wasn't any politics in it."

"Sure, but you must have said something about somebody along the way."

"Not at all. Apparently it was because of the words."

"Words? What kind of words?"

"Normal stuff, the kinds of things you say when you're arguing with someone or walking down the street. 'Fuck you, asshole'—that kind of thing."

The police officers would purse their lips at this, then walk away.

One time, on a routine transfer, a very senior commander in the security apparatus stopped the van I was in as it was about to leave. First he ordered the cadets and conscripts to hose down the whole vehicle, inside and out, yelling at them that neglecting ministry property was a disgraceful waste of resources. Then he turned to me, took off his sunglasses, and asked, dead serious: "Do you think Naguib Mahfouz used to smoke hashish?"

I was sure the correct answer to this question was that he'd almost certainly tried it, but in the context, I felt like I'd be squealing on Naguib Mahfouz if I said that. These are crazy times, I thought; I've been in prison for a while now and who knows what's going on out there—maybe they're trying to frame Mahfouz, or his ghost, on some drug charge. I mumbled something and then fell silent again. But the commander, his epaulets heavy with golden swords, gestured for me to continue.

"I couldn't say, sir," I finally ventured.

"You couldn't say! And you call yourself a writer and a journalist. I'll tell you. Listen. Hashish expands the mind. Drugs in general are good for the imagination. That's what made him able to invent all those fictional worlds he wrote about—I mean, take the character Si al-Sayyid, for example, and Amina. That takes imagination. Hashish gives you ideas. That said, everyone smokes hashish, but not everyone can write, or do half of what Naguib Mahfouz did."

I made a show of amazement at this penetrating insight, because after three hundred days in prison, I'd come to know the employees of the Ministry of the Interior very well and perfected the arts of brownnosing and ass-kissing that were generally required. This was especially the case with the higher ranks, so I went one step further and asked the commander if he himself had any literary inclinations. The answer was predictable.

The junior officers, cadets, and other prisoners gawked in amazement, wondering who on earth I was to be exchanging jokes and pleasantries with the commander in the shiny uniform carrying a walkie-talkie. There was a painful pressure on my kidneys and bladder, but for twenty minutes, I stood chatting with the commander about his love of writing and the joy of imagination.

"The joy of imagination," he repeated several times, extending his fingers and gesturing upward every time he said it, "is the highest of all the pleasures of the mind, and more enduring than all the pleasures of the body." I nodded, trying not to think about the transient physical pleasures his sagging, distended old man's body might have enjoyed, and focusing instead on those abiding pleasures of the mind.

"I had a stab at literature myself, when I was younger," he went on, "but the demands of my work life forced me to give it up. I'm waiting for my retirement so I can return to writing. I have thousands of stories to tell. I've got some brilliant ideas for TV shows too—I could write dozens of them."

We wished each other success in our literary careers, then went our separate ways—the commander to oversee his department, and me, in handcuffs, back into the van.

Day 74: Wednesday, May 4, 2016

The justice system bears no relation to justice whatsoever, either here in Egypt or in any other human society. Justice is just a metaphor the justice system likes to borrow—the same way the nation likes to use motherhood as a metaphor.

There are three pillars of resistance: imagination, faith, and trust in salvation.

Day 77: Saturday, May 7, 2016

The cellblock was in a state of agitation and fear when we woke up this morning. A Prisons Authority inspection. Roll call was held, and each person left the cell when their name was announced. Our cellmate A, who lost an eye in the blessed revolution of January 25, was stopped by an officer as he left the cell. "Why are you squinting like that? What are you hiding in there?" snapped the officer. "Nothing, sir," answered A. "I have no eye."

They lined us up on the walkway and ordered us to squat, ensuring our knees didn't touch the floor. One guy made the mistake of resting his ass on the floor for a minute, and when the officer noticed, he slapped him in the face and made him stand facing the wall with his arms above his head, like a naughty pupil being punished at school.

We were kept like that for hours. They didn't let us go to the bathroom, or drink anything, or stretch our legs, which were soon stiff and numb. The place was a trash heap when we were finally ordered back to the cellblock. Our clothes had been taken out of our bags and tossed onto the floor, and the garbage cans had been emptied on top of them. The cotton pillows some people had managed to smuggle in had been slashed open with knives, and their stuffing scattered across the cell. There were footprints and cigarette butts all over the bunks where we slept. I gathered up my belongings wearily. They'd confiscated all our glass drinking cups, our razor blades and shavers, our playing cards, and any colorful civilian clothes they could find.

RHINOCEROS TEARS

UNTIL I WENT TO PRISON, I NEVER saw myself as a writer. Occasional journalist, day laborer in the media market, often unemployed intellectual masturbator, three-legged chair, daydreamer, mental adolescent, but writer? Not sure. I was only thirty, I hadn't decided what I wanted yet, and I didn't see any reason why I should.

More than once, the question "What if?" came up—in my own mind and, presumably, in those of others too. What if I hadn't done this or that? What if I hadn't written, hadn't published? Lying sleepless in my bunk, I went over it a million times: If somehow it had occurred to me that *Using Life* would land me in prison, then I would never have written it. Writing wasn't worth this kind of sacrifice. I should have kept publishing online under a pseudonym and been satisfied with that.

Once, about eight months in, I woke up in the middle of the night needing to pee. I went to the toilet, and in the corner of the bathroom I found the Rhinoceros, crying. He raised a hand to hide his tears behind his cigarette smoke. No one had seen the Rhinoceros cry. He was famously arrogant and unfeeling, his greed and ambition proverbial. We were all familiar with his catchphrase "I'm just being an asshole to make you look good." So when I found him in tears, I knew we were dealing with a calamity of epic proportions. Out of curiosity more than pity, I went toward him and asked in a whisper if everything was okay.

Choking on his tears, he muttered that he was fine.

"Why are you crying if you're fine?"

"It's my feelings, man. They're too much for me. I need to get them out."

I was taken aback and tried again. He asked me if I'd ever read *In My Heart a Hebrew Girl*.

"No," I said, "and I don't plan to." (It's a best-selling novel in a genre you might call "Islamic romance.") The Rhinoceros told me he was in the middle of reading it.

"It's a mind-blowing book. Mind-blowing. So powerful."

I wasn't sure what this had to do with his crying, but he went on, telling me that parts of the book had moved him so much he couldn't help weeping. Even the sight of the front cover had him in tears. Ultimately, he'd had to leave the book on his bunk and come in here to fix himself up.

For the next three evenings, I watched as the Rhinoceros spoke of nothing else to our cellmates. Several times he tried unsuccessfully to convince me to read the book—although I did flick through it at one point to see if I could figure out why it had made him cry. But there was no secret to the novel; the secret was somewhere else. I saw for the first time that words, books, and literature had an inner force, a hidden strength that might be stored inside a sentence or a word or a letter. It was something weightier than simply the pleasure of reading, something superior to moralizing and edifying. As transparent as a drop of water, it was too insubstantial to be grasped, yet powerful enough to reduce the Rhinoceros's heart to crumbs.

On the fourth night, I decided to be a writer.

Day 16: Monday, March 7, 2016

One guy here has served just under three years of pretrial detention: thirty-four months exactly. Today he returned from court, bursting with joy, to be greeted with congratulations from the whole cellblock: the judge had sentenced him—finally—to three years. He doesn't know if he'll be released immediately, since he's served over two-thirds of his sentence, or be made to wait two more months. It doesn't matter much. He's so happy you'd think he'd been acquitted. Thanks to changes in the law on preventive detention, everyone here dreams of becoming a convicted criminal just so they'll know where they stand. Now and then, someone says to me, in the middle of a conversation, "You're so lucky. At least you know how long you're here. We're stuck. Before every hearing date you get your hopes up and then they're destroyed again."

I just finished *A Cat and a Mouse on the Train* by Fathy Ghanem. It's about a defeated Nasserite being chased by a mouse that embodies all the evils of the world—evils that Nasser fools him into believing in. Boring as hell, like everything from the '60s.

Day 17: Tuesday, March 8, 2016

Today, via a cellmate, I received a small visit bag containing some food, a letter from my brother Mohamed, and another from Yasmine. Finally it's like I can feel their touch. We organized a chess tournament for the cellblock chess lovers. Someone managed to smuggle in the pieces and a sheet of paper we can use for a board.

Day 19: Thursday, March 10, 2016

I dreamed I was hiding out in my old family home, looking at the internet, when suddenly Sh. warned me not to use any of my usual online accounts, so people would think I was still in prison. No one knew I'd escaped.

We've had a batch of fresh fish in the cell. It's hot and suffocating, and the summer stickiness makes you feel like your balls are in your nose. The new guys are sleeping on the floor in the passageway, piled up on top of one another in the kitchen and toilet area, and standing up against the walls. I spend the whole day sitting on my bunk. I don't get down at all. I'm reading Khairy Shalaby's Amali trilogy, and I practically laugh out loud at his description of the merry jail where the prisoners smoke hash from a homemade bong, while I inhale the smoke of dusty Cleopatras and yearn for a breath of oxygen that doesn't smell of phlegm, flatulence, and moldering food.

THE HEAD NABATSHI

I AWOKE ONE MORNING TO an unbearable stench. By about two months in, my nose had got used to the various odors produced by my cellmates, and from time to time I even amused myself by identifying the source of a fart by its smell. But this was no human odor; it was the unmistakable reek of decomposition coming from the direction of the kitchen and the toilets.

Every cellblock ended in a section that housed a row of toilet stalls on the left and a kitchen on the right. This "kitchen" consisted of a concrete workbench roughly a meter high, with a recessed area where three or four electric heating coils were attached to a single main dial. When switched on, the coils would heat up; a metal grille was placed over the top, and the cooking vessels rested on this. Next to this rudimentary stove was a washbowl, which we used for both dishwashing and for washing our faces.

We stacked the plastic and aluminum dining plates underneath the sink, where they were picked over by cockroaches and other insects. Each toilet stall was covered by a plastic curtain, since doors were banned. Washing lines were strung across this entire section of the cellblock, so just-washed boxer shorts and white and blue shirts could be hung out to dry in the warm vapors of rancid cooking oil and the shit-scented steam that rose out of the open toilet holes.

But the stench that woke me that morning wasn't any of the familiar foul smells that emanated from the kitchen-toilet area. I raised my head from the pillow as I breathed in. The density of the odor in the air made me hold my breath; with every mouthful of air, I could feel the poisonous particles making their way into my body, turning my stomach, and curling my intestines, so I felt like I was about to throw up my own shit. I reached out for my bottle of water and lifted it to drink, but even the water was contaminated with the smell. I looked around me. Half the cell was still asleep, but those who were awake had all covered their noses with fabric.

"Boss, what's the smell?" I called out to the nabatshi.

"No idea," he called back from behind the curtains that shielded his lower bunk. "Somebody's got some food in their bunk and it's gone bad, I guess."

I couldn't stand it. I got out of bed and headed for the kitchen. Here, I was in the eye of the storm. Until this moment I'd never known what effect the smell of decomposition could have on the human body, but now tears were streaming uncontrollably from my eyes. I was forced to sniff to work out where the stench was coming from, quickly realizing that the culprit was a blue trash can, one of three in the cellblock.

Several others had to come to help. We found that the source of the smell was half a pan of zucchini in tomato sauce going moldy at the bottom of the trash can. It was part of the prison food they'd given us the day before, and since it was rotten when it arrived, no one had eaten it. It had been thrown into the trash, where it had continued its rotting process. To make matters worse, all the trash had been dumped into the can without a liner, so we couldn't pull the spoiled food out. We would have to wait until 10:00 a.m., when the trash was collected from the cellblocks.

All this had happened because we were out of trash bags. The nabatshi was waiting for his weekly visit, when his family would bring the kilo's worth of liners he'd asked them to buy from the Maadi branch of Carrefour, where they were cheaper than the rolls you could get in the prison cafeteria. The nabatshi claimed in his defense that he was trying to be economical with cellblock money—the irony of this being that he was a senior civil servant charged with accepting bribes and misusing public funds.

It was the nabatshi's responsibility to manage the affairs of the cellblock, or, in a police precinct, the detention cell. The nabatshi allocated bunks, determined amounts of personal space, ensured prison regulations were obeyed, and served as the final arbiter in any disputes.

With his deputy, the nabatshi also assigned a group of inmates to cleaning duty, which consisted of mopping the floors with bleach at least twice a day, in exchange for a salary of cigarettes (paid for by the charges the nabatshi levied on the others).

You either paid others with cigarettes or worked in exchange for them. This was the prison's class structure, and it was carefully maintained by the nabatshis, who had to ensure a balance within each cellblock of those who were able to pay and those who were prepared to serve. Working inmates could sell their cigarettes at the cafeteria for credit that could be used to buy their own food. This way they didn't have to depend on prison rations or the standard-issue meals that we refused to eat—apart from the two pieces of meat, distributed on Mondays and Thursdays, to which we were entitled. Inmates who were worse off would request work in the prison factory or volunteer for extra service duties within the cellblock, like laundry or cleaning bunks, in exchange for more packs of cigarettes, which they'd pass on to their families at visiting time so they could be sold for money on the outside. In this manner, the prisoner was able to continue supporting their family.

Each prison had a cafeteria, which was overseen by an inmate, often the one who'd been there the longest. The cafeteria nabatshi was the third most powerful figure in the prison, after the warden and the chief of intelligence, which explained why he was also known simply as the "head nabatshi." Prison regulations permitted cafeterias to make a profit margin of up to 25 percent, which was distributed by the nabatshi among those who ran the prison—meaning he controlled the amount of extra cash the guards themselves would earn. The nabatshi also set the price of a pack of cigarettes, thereby controlling the value of prison currency. It was as if he were the head of the prison's central bank, and as such his powers were many and wide-ranging. Thanks to his relationship with the warden and the authorities, he could turn the prison—if they let him—into a five-star hotel or a hell for inmates and guards alike.

At one point, a new senior officer showed up. He was soft around the edges, had a cute little paunch, and apparently also had a weakness for fast food. The nabatshi quickly put in an order for hot dog buns with the prison's food supplier, bought a griddle and deep fryer for the french fries, just like they use at fast-food joints, and was soon doing a roaring trade in hot dogs and hamburgers. The officer was pretty happy because he got to eat this stuff for free, but sadly it couldn't last, and the chief of intelligence swiftly intervened to end these otherworldly pleasures.

But the nabatshi's powers of procurement didn't stop at cooking supplies; he was also in charge of ordering the tools and spare parts required to perform any maintenance required in the cellblocks. At one point, for example, we managed to buy a water heater so we could have hot showers, and when the electric pump burned out, it was the nabatshi who was able to get hold of the part we needed to fix it. And of course, if you were in the nabatshi's good books, you could procure many other things, too, whether they were permitted or not.

BLANKET

I LIT A CIGARETTE AND leaned against the metal railing of the walkway that looked out over the yard and the first-floor cellblocks. It was recreation hour, and the heat and humidity were suffocating. A strange, somber mood enveloped the cellblock, replacing the habitual hum of conversation with silence.

Thinking that things seemed different from usual, I registered that none of the cell doors were open and none of the inmates had come out for recreation. A plainclothes officer emerged from one of the cells below, followed by four prisoners, each gripping one corner of a dirty standard-issue blanket. Lying in the blanket was the unmoving body of a prisoner. Naked from the waist up, the body was pale and grayish; a sheet of newspaper lay over the face. I followed the cortege from above as it transported the new corpse out into the world.

It wasn't the first time I'd seen a dead body, but it was the first time I'd seen one treated with such contempt, such indifference to death. There was no screaming or weeping, and I heard no one reciting the two shahadas. The guard was pissed off and cursing foully because it was going to mean paperwork, which he hated.

"Your life is worth twenty pounds here" was a threat I'd often heard repeated by the lieutenants and guards. Twenty pounds was the cost of the standard-issue blanket in which they would wrap your dead body and send you back to your family.

Day 70: Saturday, April 30, 2016

Dreamed I was in a restaurant. I was the only customer. The bartender brought a tiny dead bird marinated in spices and placed it on a coal grill, and when the meat was done, he fetched a martini glass and squeezed the bird in his fist so the fat drizzled into the glass. He squeezed harder and the bird's flesh oozed out in a thick liquid and filled the glass. He placed the bird—now a mess of crushed bone and flesh—on the table. With a large knife he shredded it into minuscule strips, added them to the glass, and invited me to drink.

THE FIXER

ON DAY TWO IN PRISON I was taking an afternoon nap when a hand shook me awake. I opened my eyes to see a prisoner dressed in white, with elegantly combed hair and a TV smile. He wasn't one of ours. He put a black plastic bag down on my bunk and leaned forward to whisper, "This is from Alaa." I looked inside the bag and found a white T-shirt, ten packs of cigarettes, and a towel. It was a welcome gift from one of the prison's most high-profile political prisoners, Alaa Abd el-Fattah, who was in the cellblock just next door. "You can order stuff on Alaa's account in the cafeteria," the man added, "and if you need anything else, just let me know." As I soon found out, this man with the good hair was one of the prison's "fixers."

Like the warden, the chief of intelligence, and the nabatshi, the fixer was one of the pillars of prison administration. Fixers were usually inmates who'd had a university education and were always well-groomed and well-spoken. They formed a crucial link between the authorities and the prisoners.

A fixer would get up at 7:00 a.m., before the prison's civilian employees arrived. He would shower and get dressed in his prison uniform and sneakers, which made the task of running errands around the prison all day long much more comfortable. At eight, a guard would open the cellblock and the fixer would go downstairs to start work in an office in the administrative section.

The fixer's office in our prison contained a battered Louis XIV–style wooden bureau, three leather chairs, some filing cabinets, and a bookcase of the kind you see behind the reception desk in old hotels. Maybe that was because the fixer's job was actually pretty similar to that of a hotel receptionist, except that his filing cabinets contained not keys to bedrooms, but the inmates' identity cards.

Upon arrival, every prisoner was given a card that showed their name, offense, sentence, release date, and visit dates. These cards lived in boxes, grouped by cellblock, in the fixer's office. Your placement within the prison reflected where your ID was stored, and if the fixer was told by the chief of intelligence to move a card from 1/4 to 2/3, you, too, would swiftly be moved from cellblock 1/4 to 2/3. On visiting days, the fixer would be informed which inmates were scheduled to receive visits, and because he knew which cellblock they were accommodated in, it was he who would personally tell each inmate when visiting time was coming up, so they could dress and get ready to go out.

But in addition to serving in an administrative capacity, fixers were double agents that looked out onto both worlds— that of the guards and that of the inmates. They moved freely between the two, earning the trust of both sides. They returned to their cellblock a little after 5:00 p.m., when all the civilian administrators had left for the day. If you had a complaint, they were your first port of call, and if they couldn't help you, they would know who could.

Day 86: Monday, May 16, 2016

I spend the whole day feeling nauseated, exhausted, and fed up. My nose runs constantly in the suffocating heat and humidity, and the medication I'm taking for my cold is sapping my strength and making my sweat smell like antibiotics. I feel like throwing up the whole time, but there's nothing in my stomach to throw up.

Today the guys called me over during the nine o'clock news, which was reporting on a cabinet decision regarding new legislation covering the media. The shitty part is that although they've agreed that the bill needs to be amended because it violates press freedoms and conflicts with several articles in the new constitution, they've postponed making the amendments. Then there was another news item saying the Ministry of Justice has appointed a committee to write the amendments. Needless to say, if these amendments happen, then it won't just mean I get out of prison; it will mean that everything that's happened has some meaning.

It's impossible to know what's going on outside from the TV reports, but at least something is happening. The wheel is creaking slowly into motion. It isn't going anywhere yet, but at least it's moving. Or am I just getting my hopes up for nothing?

THE POWER OF "AH"

ONE DAY, A RURAL BUSINESSMAN with investments in the ball-park of ten million Egyptian pounds showed up in the cellblock and spent the next three weeks with us, having foolishly taken part in some small-time scam. I was up late reading by lamplight, with everyone else in the cellblock asleep, when I heard his sobs and looked over to see him curled up on his bunk, muttering incomprehensibly to himself in despair. The only sentence I could make out was "Mom, I wish you were here."

The businessman's crying barely made a sound—it was just a repeated whimper of "Ah... ah... ah...," interspersed with the same plea: "Mom, I wish you were here." He kept it together during the day; he spent most of his time swapping anecdotes with the other guys and telling the story of his case—which always emphasized his innocence—to anyone who would listen. But in the dark of night, he had nobody to console him. His lament was most audible when he called out to his mom—this gray-haired man, who'd boasted to his cellmates about fighting in the second Gulf War, wanted nothing more than to return to his mother's womb in order to escape the misery of prison—but when his desperation was at its deepest, he'd return to the same plaintive "ah," which he repeated over and over until the early hours of the morning.

Late one evening another prisoner finally snapped. "That's enough, man," he yelled at him. "We're all sick and tired."

This particular guy was not averse to complaints; out of all our cellmates, he was actually one of the kindest and friendliest, with a real knack for drawing people out of their private sadness. He never got bored of listening to the minutiae of people's trials and always found a way to comfort them, cursing the people who'd put them here or making light of their mistakes and turning their gloomy prospects into a joke even they could laugh at. But faced with that pathetic "ah," there was nothing he could do. There was nothing any of us could do to cheer him up or get him to stop; it was useless even to object.

That was the terrible power of his wordless, unreachable despair. Neither spoken nor silent, the "ah" filled the air in the cellblock, sucking out its oxygen. We were held captive by that "ah," a tongue-tied chorus standing motionless behind it.

VEXING

AFTER THE FIRST MONTH, MY living conditions improved. I managed to get hold of a thin mattress, about five centimeters thick, and placed a blanket underneath it to separate it from the damp concrete surface of the bunk. I established a strict daily routine and stuck to it, because any gaps in activity made the time stretch out and drag. I started receiving visitors: seeing Yasmine, my mom, and my brother Mohamed—and being able to give them a hug—filled me with a renewed desire for life, and gave me a regular dose of fresh hope.

The most important parts of the day were the sessions I spent doing the crossword and sudoku, because they took up so much time, followed by the hours I spent reading. But as summer settled in, the heat and humidity in the cellblock intensified, and it felt constantly disgusting to be around myself. I'd lie on my right side with a book, trying to lose myself in the adventures of

Vladimir Nabokov's *Lolita*, until I could feel sweat pooling on the small pillow and would have to get up and change positions. The pillow absorbed sweat very quickly, and the only solution was to flip the mattress or pillow over, which would give you a brief reprieve before that side, too, was soaked. From June to August it got so bad that I'd have to regularly remove the pillow from its case to wring out the sweat, and wrap a towel around it to stop it from becoming totally saturated.

The constant struggle with heat and humidity entailed numerous secondary battles. For example, the refrigerator we used for water was opened only three times per day, so you'd spend hours waiting for that sacred moment when the nabatshi finally handed you a bottle of cold water. And you could take a shower—which would momentarily liberate you from the stink of your own sweat—only when the water pressure was strong enough.

But summer didn't truly sink its claws in until holiday season, when the authorities would be on standby to "vex" us, if there was trouble, or if one of the intelligence guys got pissed. Vexing was first explained to me by two old-timers, an inmate and a guard, as we stood smoking a cigarette together one day. The prison administration's main aim, they said, was to prevent inmates from "using their brains" against those around them, be they guards or other inmates, because that was how trouble started, escape plans were hatched, and rules were broken. There were fewer guards on duty during religious festivals and national holidays, and these blessed days would naturally make prisoners think about their families and loved ones and the sad predicament they were in, leaving them restless and liable to lose their temper with one another. And so on these types of occasions, the prison could be "vexed" using a couple of simple methods.

During my first Eid in prison, we went without running water for three days. There was usually water for an hour and a half per day, during which inmates scrambled to fill their buckets and the bottles they drank from. Because I had kidney problems, I made sure to drink mineral water rather than water out of the faucet; I was among the lucky few who could afford to. We'd each buy a boxful of one-liter bottles to last us the week, but during that waterless Eid, I handed out all my remaining bottles. We were thirsty, and the smell of shit and piss and sweat and mold issued forcefully from the kitchen and lavatory area. The entire prison was on lockdown for the duration of the holiday, so the trash bags containing our rotting food waste sat in the cellblock with us for three days straight.

For those three days we thought of nothing but water. I fell asleep hoping I'd dream of water, of drinking, of being sated, but the dream didn't come. Remembering that it was Eid only made it worse. When they decided to vex us, there was no thinking, no using our brains: our single, all-consuming obsession was the desperate urge to drink and to piss.

SURROUNDED BY CHARRED BODIES, MY FATHER CRIED

ONE DAY, THE FORMER ARMY officer who shared my cell and demanded that we address him as "General," decided to spend three hours proudly recounting the role he'd played in the operation to clear the Rabaa Square sit-in. During that incident, around a thousand civilians, who were taking part in a protest against the ouster of then president Mohamed Morsi, were massacred. The General was a lying skunk and I could tell that he wanted to provoke me; he was watching my facial expressions like a hawk, trying to work out what my political position was, while he boasted about the crimes against humanity they'd committed that day.

My father was there at Rabaa. I still remember the day of the massacre. It was my mother who woke me up, calling to tell me she couldn't get in touch with my dad. She said he'd left early to go to Cairo, and now the police were storming Rabaa.

I checked the news and my Twitter timeline. The army and the police were preparing to disperse the sit-in. After I'd tried several times to get through to him, my father finally answered his phone. His voice was calm; he told me he'd left the area and everything was fine. On the TV screen, Rabaa Square looked like a battlefield, but there was no real battle: only soldiers marching over charred bodies.

In fact, my father was lying so I wouldn't worry about him. He had indeed been at the square during the massacre. When he later told me what he'd witnessed, he wept. He's a pediatrician, so when the assault started, he immediately tried to help. Several people died in his arms. Other Muslim Brotherhood protesters were taking the dead bodies and placing them in a tent, and during one of the attacks, the army burned this tent, with all the dead bodies inside. When my father saw the flames engulfing the tent-cum-morgue, he decided it was time to leave. By some miracle, he was able to get out.

Over the following weeks, my father fell into a deep sadness and depression. We would be eating, and suddenly he'd stop, his spoon halfway to his mouth. If I asked him what was wrong, all he wanted to talk about was charred bodies, or the faces of the young people and teenagers pleading for help while he searched for cloths to stop their bleeding.

Then, two months later, my father left his job, house, and country, and resolved never to return. Even during the year I spent in prison, he visited me only once—and he came then, I found out, only because he'd had a heart attack. Regardless of the security consequences he faced as a Brotherhood member, he knew he needed to see his eldest son, who was learning how to contain himself and fake a smile while he listened to the officer's stories about all the people he'd killed at Rabaa.

Day 22: Sunday, March 13, 2016

Day in, day out, the wind batters the huge metal barrier that separates our prison from the Agricultural Prison. They put it up because Alaa and Gamal Mubarak are held next door in the Agricultural, and inmates here used to wait until they came out on rec and then scream insults at them over the fence. So it's thanks to the Mubarak family that we have to listen to the sound of the wind but never get to feel the fresh air it brings.

At rec hour today the sky was yellow. It's the season of the khamasin, the nightmarish desert wind that engulfs the whole of Cairo. I think that at least I don't have to spend the next few days sweeping sand and dust from every surface in the house, my sinuses burning.

There's a religious revolution brewing in the cellblock. An engineer charged with taking bribes has started getting a group of inmates together and giving lessons in Qur'an and religious studies. A couple of days back he swore to one of our cellmates that he would write an exegesis of the Qur'an that fixed all the mistakes that Shaykh Sha'rawi—the most popular preacher in Egypt—had made in his interpretation. The engineer has taken a bunch of wretched draft dodgers, most of them so poor they never finished high school—they're the only

ones willing to listen to the crap he spouts, and take the cigarettes he bribes them with—and turned them into a cultlike
band of followers, warning them that anyone who doesn't read
the Qur'an is an infidel. At one point they started refusing to
eat food cooked by the cellblock chef, because he's supposedly
a heathen, and an aggressive jurisprudential debate broke
out between the chef and the engineer, sprinkled, of course,
with plenty of blasphemous insults. It got so heated that the
nabatshi stepped in and forced the engineer to apologize to the
chef and the rest of the cellblock.

TEDDY BEARS

STATUS, INFLUENCE, AND ECONOMIC PRIVILEGE didn't disappear in prison. Prison simply reassembled the social classes into the same hierarchy that existed on the outside.

At the end of visiting hours, I'd always find a handful of young inmates hovering, ready to help carry the bags I'd been given, and since there were usually a lot of bags, I surrendered willingly to their offers. In exchange for carrying these bags back to the cellblock, I would give each one a pack of cigarettes. In reality, you couldn't really refuse their offers; otherwise, they'd think you were stingy. If God had been generous with you, then you ought to kick back and relax and pay others to do the hard work for you.

Offers streamed in from poorer inmates, Egyptian and foreign alike, and those who had no visitors to bring them food, clothes, or other things they needed. Their services were varied:

they could air and change your bedlinen, for example, or scrub your bunk, or be on hand to prepare drinks when you wanted. I didn't like the term, but they were known as "teddy bears." As with everything else, you paid for the teddy bears' services in packs of cigarettes and maybe also shared your food with them. I tried to think of the teddy bear system as a crude form of social welfare, but I also saw cases where the relationship between teddy bear and "pasha"—a term that designated the wealthy inmates—was one of socioeconomic exploitation, pure and simple.

One of the pashas in my cell had a Brazilian teddy bear, a young man who was in for drug-smuggling offenses. The young Brazilian cleaned the pasha's bunk every day with a mix of bleach and Dettol to kill fleas and cockroaches, while the pasha stood over him watching, pointing out corners he'd missed and barking instructions in a mix of Arabic and English, adding hand gestures when the message wasn't getting through. One day they began to argue over the bill: the Brazilian teddy bear insisted he was owed four packs of cigarettes, while the Egyptian pasha refused to hand over more than two. The Brazilian was holding a mug of tea as this argument unfolded, and finally, furious and having given up hope of resolving things amicably with his stingy Egyptian boss, he emptied the mug over a copy of Shaykh Sha'rawi's commentary on the Qur'an, which lay open on the pasha's bunk.

The pasha lost his shit. He picked up the tea-sodden volume and waved it aloft, screaming the shahada at the top of his lungs as he strode around the cellblock. "He's throwing tea on the words of our Lord!" he shouted. "He's insulting our God! You'd better make him pay for this, Nabatshi!"

There's an Islamic saying, "Pay the worker his due before his sweat has dried." But the pasha's refusal to pay meant that a dispute over two packs of cigarettes had turned into angry sectarian strife that would have gotten out of hand, had a group of our cellmates not intervened to calm things down.

Conflict could kick off in the cellblock without any warning, but it could also quickly peter out, and relationships between inmates would return to normal. Three days later I saw the Brazilian teddy bear back at work, spraying down the pasha's bunk while the latter stood watching, happy to return to his role of feudal overseer.

Day 139: Friday, July 8, 2016

I dreamed I traveled back in time and became a women's hairdresser in the 1940s, except that I had tools and techniques from the future, which amazed my clients and made me hugely in demand. My clients came from the most distinguished upper-class families, and through my work I met a young, wealthy couple who were deeply unhappy. I offered my services to the wife, and the groom quickly became convinced I had the power to save their marriage.

I took all my products from the future to our appointment—relaxer, gel, hair spray—and styled her hair, then asked her to lie down naked on her front.

"Relax," I urged her as I massaged her shoulders. I knew the husband was hiding somewhere, spying on us, and I deliberately worked my way down her back until I was kneading her bare buttocks. My cock became painfully erect, but I continued my work until the tips of my fingers felt her wetness, and then asked the maid to call the husband.

The husband entered the bedroom and I stepped out, but my spirit remained hovering over the couple, encouraging them to rediscover their love and desire. I went to the bathroom and attempted to relieve the tension and pain of my erection, but what finally exploded into the washbowl was a stream of black liquid that shimmered like petroleum.

KEEPING CLEAN

EVERY ONCE IN A WHILE, after prayers in the afternoon or evening, the nabatshi would stand up and reiterate some cellblock rules or discuss some issues that had come up recently. Rules were repeated for the benefit of any new prisoners, or "intake"; as he went through them, I always listened closely to make sure he remembered the most important point, and if he didn't, I'd raise my hand. "Boss, don't forget about the soap buckets and the toilets."

Of the five toilets in the cellblock, just two were "European-style," and the other three were "local-style"—essentially little more than a hole in the ground. Even in the European toilets, the flusher didn't work most of the time. The solution was to fill a bucket with water and drop in a small piece of standard-issue soap, and some bleach or Dettol, too, when times were good. One of these buckets was kept inside every stall, and whenever you took a leak or a dump, you'd use it to throw some soapy water down the toilet bowl so its stinking remains didn't sit there for the rest of the day.

But one morning, I entered a toilet stall to find a large, heavy turd, not inside the toilet bowl, but sitting right there on the tiled floor. It was pyramid-shaped and slightly dried, and three flies were hovering above it while a little lost cockroach scuttled in circles around it. I turned straight around and went to wake the nabatshi.

"Look at this, boss," I said, dragging him to the lavatory stall in question. "I hope you're going to find out who's been packing before we all get in trouble."

What we were looking at was clear evidence of wrongdoing; we just didn't know by whom. A turd on the floor could mean only that someone had been packing contraband in their ass, most likely drugs, and didn't want to evacuate in the toilet until they'd recovered all the pills or whatever it was they'd smuggled in. So there was contraband in the cellblock now, and it would surface sooner or later, which meant they'd vex us and take all our luxuries away, from the TV right down to the refrigerators.

The nabatshi stood in the middle of the cellblock to deliver a long monologue on the vile scene with which we'd just been confronted. We were respectable men who shouldn't behave like that; whoever was responsible was hurting the whole cellblock; and so on. Then he asked the person in question to get rid of the contraband so we didn't all have to bear the consequences.

"Every one of us here is responsible for keeping clean," he concluded gravely.

No one came forward, and we never found out who had been packing.

Day 157: Tuesday, July 26, 2016

Whenever we hear the call to prayer—which streams in from the city outside—the observant line themselves up in the open space between the bunks, and Uncle G goes to his bunk. I watch from above as he takes out his Bible and wooden rosary and begins to pray. He does this four times each day—every time the Muslims pray—and sometimes, if he happens to be awake late anyway, he even joins them for the dawn prayer. According to my limited knowledge, it's usually only Muslims who pray five times a day. I've considered asking him the no-doubt-invasive question about why he prays so much, but I don't want to make his life more of a pain in the ass than it already is.

In our cellblock, like everywhere else in prison, there's a latent tension between Muslims and Christians, but Uncle G is a curious case. He doesn't seem to get annoyed like the other Christians do by how the Muslims block the only passageway in the cellblock at prayer times, and he doesn't object to the strictures of Ramadan, or any other inconveniences imposed by living with a Muslim majority. Instead, he piously observes his rituals, which have a Christian aura and yet a heretical essence, straying as they do so far beyond the Church's commandments.

LAUGHTER AND RAGE

FINALLY I WAS ABLE TO SEE a copy of the court's reasoning. Yasmine brought it with her on one of her visits: seven pages in which the president of the court of appeals evaluated the evidence, explained his ruling, and justified the two-year prison sentence. When the visit was over, I slowly made my way back to the cellblock, lit a cigarette, and sat down to read. Waves of anger surged through me with every line I read. The only way I could deal with it was to laugh. There were so many typos I often had to stop to re-read a sentence. This is how it went:

> Safeguarding the family which is the basis of society takes precedence over protecting the interests of the individual or the sector of society which has no concern but to protect itself from punishment and keep themselves safe from any sanctions which would restrict their

freedom, claiming freedom of opinion and creativity, but what creativity is there in the writing of the defendant, which is filled with language that offends public dignity and incites depravity and vice.

The author of the constitution, when writing article 67 of the constitution, which concerns freedom of literary and artistic expression, did not intend to protect those who purport to be writers and yet spread vice and sin upon the earth and corrupt morals with their poisoned pens under the pretense of freedom of thought, otherwise he would contradict himself in having legislated to protect the family because it is the basis of society and to protect religion and morals.

My friends in the cellblock hurried over to take a look. A former judge accused of taking bribes took the papers from me and began to read out loud, but he was soon laughing so hard at how badly it was written that he could barely get through a paragraph.

By writing, the first defendant may have utilized his right as granted to him by the constitution and the law, but that is conditional upon it remaining within the bounds of the law and not aiming to use that right for other than legal purposes, as the defendant has done by writing what he calls the novel *Using Life*, which employs words and expressions which are offensive to public morality, centering on the depiction of an act of vice between a man and a woman and treating details of that act in a manner which ignores the values and traditions and mores of Egyptian society and far exceeds the bounds of freedom of expression and composition granted by the constitution which aims to elevate the nation, foster morals and manners and encourage people to abide by them.

That paragraph was my favorite, because it revealed what my real crime was, in the judge's view. It wasn't anything to do with "offensive expressions" or depicting a man and woman wallowing in vice. My real transgression was to have deliberately ignored the values and mores of Egyptian society—which I freely admit I've always hated and despised. I had taken every available opportunity to spit on its values and piss on its mores, and I'd shit on the whole damn thing if I could. And I was happy to say that my writing certainly didn't aim to elevate the nation or foster morals and manners. I wanted to encourage people to take a good look at this thing we called a nation, to think long and hard about it, and if that meant they might want to run as far away from it as they could, or burn it to the ground, then so be it. I didn't have anything to offer to society. I just found that writing was a way of knowing and understanding myself—and a way of getting to know you, whoever you are, you who are reading this now. I found my voice through writing and through your reading, and in the words we shared, I found a meaning to life that seemed bigger than the nation-state, with its flag and its anthem and its army and its museums and its schools and its national literature, which was supposed to drag people up to some purported cosmic standard of good manners and morals.

My cellmates stood in a circle in front of me, passing the document around and taking turns reading it out loud. It was handed to another former judge—this one a court president, also accused of taking bribes—who flicked back through the pages he'd just heard. "This ruling isn't valid," he said calmly. "The guy's just rambling. This is just his opinion. What even is this?"

He held up three whole pages that the judge had devoted to an excursus into the meaning of literature, arrogantly attempting to define anew the craft of novel writing.

> The court notes in preparing its ruling that the linguistic origin of the word "literature," adab, is an invitation to food, and by extension, the person who performs adab extends a call to virtuous acts, to the adornment of the self with good morals, and to the performance of commendable deeds, and aims to impart knowledge and improve behaviors, and hence the writer of literature, the adib, is the tongue of society, truthfully expressing its hopes, and of the Islamic nation, so that he may earn society's acceptance, but regrettably literature is in crisis, not only as regards itself, it's styles of language,

it's meanings and the aims of it's meanings [*sic*], but also as regards those responsible for it and their methods and persuasions.

The novel is one of the arts of literature, and the most popular, having a huge influence over society, in that it deals with human experiences and situations in a given time and place and provides advice and a moral, or a story and a lesson, which benefit us in our lives.

I definitely wasn't the "tongue of society," and I didn't want to "earn its acceptance." In fact, I couldn't see how a writer could "truthfully express" anything and still hope to earn social acceptance. Can society ever bear to hear the truth, as Taha Hussein asked seventy years ago? And, anyway, when did this society of ours ever get together and agree on anything? How could one book earn everybody's approval, when we were a society of two religions, each of which had its own book? And, most important, why would I want to be the tongue of society when everyone else in society had their own tongue—and if I were to be the tongue of society, then what about my own tongue?

It was all these tongues, their plurality and their diversity, that constituted my ingredients. I took their language and, yes—my literature could be an invitation to food; why not?—I turned it into a feast for two: the reader and me. Why should I be punished for using the language of my society?

In the Arabic-speaking region, the novel isn't an art form intended for the masses. It appeared in our culture as a modern alternative to poetry and to the vernacular epics that were narrated by storytellers to assembled crowds, accompanied by a stringed instrument called the rebab. The novel was a new medium that addressed the individual as he attempted to endure the loneliness of the industrial age, devouring the gods as they devoured him. It wasn't meant to set an example or have a moral; it was about subjective experience. Even in historical fiction or socialist realism, it was the author's subjective engagement with the subject matter that made the story what it was. And unlike parables and fables, which were meant to teach a lesson about life, the aim of the novel was to faithfully represent life as it was, with all its mistakes and depravities and unhappy endings and pointless "lessons" that in reality taught you nothing at all.

So I'd broken the rules. I hadn't used my freedom of expression to serve the nation and its institutions. I hadn't striven to be the tongue of society or to earn its acceptance. I hadn't written a story that had a moral or a lesson, and so the judge—and behind him the entire institution that was the country's criminal justice system—had charged me with violating tradition, abusing the novel, and insulting literature itself.

Next, the reasoning took a dubious detour into the field of rhetoric and its relationship to literature.

> Needless to say, rhetoric is one of the most important fields of the Arabic language, and it has many techniques including metonymy, allusion, and so on, and

if the defendant had been well versed in the techniques
of the Arabic language and its literature then he could
have used any one of them to express what he wished
to say as required by the context of the novel, and he
would do well to study them, for instead he chose the
most despicable vocabulary which is used only by societies devoid of morality.

All this was meant to give the ruling a veneer of literary credibility. He had really tried to establish a definition of
literature on which to base the ruling, a list of its aims and
functions and a description of how its techniques worked, and
he'd even included a bizarre array of Qur'anic quotations—on
intercourse, menstruation, plowing, marriage—to support
his argument. He then went on to apply this unique literary
criticism to my novel.

The court is satisfied, having examined the novel *Using
Life*, written in the full knowledge of the first defendant, that he used offensive words and expleetives [the
judge had actually spelled this word incorrectly] which
he repeated throughout the entire novel, admitting that
they were offensive and taking satisfaction in repeating
them throughout the novel and celebrating what he
called their "magic" in a social media post written after
the ruling at first instance; the court itself refranes [*sic*]
from repeating the words in question as to do so would

violate the sanctity of public decorum and good morals
and incite fornication and breach of propriety.

I found the judge's obsession with my humble self quite
unnerving. His newfound love of literature had taken him into
the literary world, with all its gossip, and he'd gone to the
trouble of following my social media accounts and reading all
the "expleetives" I'd written and then cited them in his ruling,
even though they weren't submitted as evidence in the trial.

As witnesses for the defense, we'd called Dr. Gaber 'Asfur,
Sonallah Ibrahim, and Muhammad Salmawi, who were novelists, professors of literature, and experts. Responding to their
testimony, the judge wrote:

> The fact that certain people approve of what the defen-
> dant wrote is not sufficient reason for permissiveness
> because the period of adolescence may be extended in
> certain people to the point that it is delayed into adult-
> hood and indeed middle age, due to total submission to
> the emotions of adolescence and the presence of vicious
> satanic nourishment, and thus it is not impossible for
> a person to become elderly of body while remaining
> adolescent in mind and psyche.

With this paragraph, the judge had managed to portray three
of the most respected living Egyptian writers as pimple-faced
teenagers who'd been overfed on "satanic nourishment." The

defamation was so overblown, it was reminiscent of the satirical poetry of al-Jahiz's time, but it conveyed very succinctly the judge's hostility toward these three literary men, their political views, and their proximity to the institutions of the state.

Gaber 'Asfur was a former minister of culture, a university professor, and a literary critic from the city of Mahalla al-Kubra. Sonallah Ibrahim, one of the most famous writers of his generation, was politically further left, but these days was accepted by the new regime and its media. And Muhammad Salmawi was a writer and former editor of *al-Ahram Hébdo*, a large French-language newspaper, who had crowned his career in public life with the position of spokesperson for the committee that wrote the 2014 constitution—the same constitution that the judge had used to rule that my behavior was a crime, calling the articles that protected freedom of opinion and expression the efforts of a sector of society "which has no concern but to protect itself from punishment." These three names represented a broad swath of writers, thinkers, and ordinary Egyptians united by a love of literature and a passionate belief in its freedom, and to a large extent they had succeeded in earning the respect of the state, even if they didn't fully share its politics.

So what did the judge's position really represent? Was it a matter of taste, or a position against the institution he represented and its support of literature and those who lived from it, because in his mind they all fed on "vicious satanic nourishment"? Was it anger at a clique that had somehow rejected him, or a deep hatred shared by all the state's institutions toward literature and its people? Or was it just about telling off a boy who'd been rude and didn't know the rules of polite language, and needed to be sent to prison to learn his lesson?

More important, what could I do now? What tools do readers and writers have at their disposal when they confront this sort of attack? How can a writer arm himself when he goes into battle?

James Joyce, who swore to express himself with the greatest degree of freedom possible—and never to serve home, father-land, or church—said a writer had three weapons: silence, exile, and cunning. Well, Joyce, they put me in prison, and all I had left was laughter and rage.

CALL TO ARMS

THE COURT CONCLUDED ITS REASONING with a call to arms addressed to legislators and others who had the country's best interests at heart:

> Before laying aside its pen, the court calls upon the leg-
> islator to review the penalties prescribed for defendants
> with a view to increasing them, because encouraging
> vice in an attempt to destroy the values of society is
> a serious matter, the commission of which must be
> dealt with with the utmost severity; the court also
> calls upon the parties responsible for the censorship of
> literary works to fight against the poison that is being
> smuggled into books, in order to arraign those who
> have committed these crimes and bring them before
> a court of law so that they may be punished for their

actions, and as a warning to those who call for freedom without restriction of religion or morality, and "do not let the reproach of any reproacher have influence on you in the path of God," or any writer with a poisoned pen or strident voice yapping on the television and satellite channels, which is heresy in itself, saying that the state is waging war on creators and thinkers this creativity and thought is wretched or those who discuss that morals are relative and subjective rather than fixed and do not have fixed truths in themselves and may be changed and substituted is it not shameful that the destiny of a nation should be left to the mercy of those who treat this destiny with disdain and impudence as if they were playing at cards and surely we have put up with enough of the cursing and swearing and insulting of individuals and institutions that we see on our television screens day in day out under the pretext of freedom this freedom is bankrupt and brings us nothing but immorality and vice and does not provide anything but moral turpitude which afflicts many people since recent events witnessed by our beloved Egypt.

With this, the train wreck of sixth-grade rhetorical skills, scandalous misspellings, nonexistent punctuation, and embarrassing grammar mistakes came to a close.

How ironic that my teachers and parents had so often violently punished me for my linguistic transgressions when I was a child. I was a distracted and careless pupil—even now I still make mistakes all the time—and I was always in trouble with the powers that be for my low scores in spelling tests. Only at the age of twenty-five did I discover by chance that I was dyslexic. And now here I was, age thirty, reading the judgment of the court that deprived me of two years of my life—one spent in Tura Prison and the other in the bigger prison of Egypt, with a travel ban against my name—and even I could see it was a linguistic horror show.

This man just wanted power, and he had been granted the right to fill page after blank page with the Arabic language, giving writers lessons in what they could and couldn't do, when he himself couldn't string together three words without a spelling mistake. The guy couldn't put a hamza in the right place to save his life, and yet because he was a judge, invested with the stupid, self-satisfied, unshakable power of the coercive apparatus that was the justice system, he was permitted to pollute the Arabic language and violate its grammar and imprison anybody who had the temerity to use it for their own purposes.

The judge exercises his power through language. He reads the submissions and evidence, analyzes words, then produces a verdict using the power of language and the numbers of laws. All judges, from all cultures and legal systems, have the same tendency to use grand, overblown language in their rulings, as if grandiloquence were capable of making their murderous decisions into clean and virtuous texts, the enactments of divine will that preserve the universal balance of all things. Just look at death sentences, and how judges weave in phrases professing that blind justice is all about right and virtue and the greater good.

And our judge clearly had hidden literary preferences, too, and bones to pick with certain literary trends, which he actually mentioned in the ruling, describing our three witnesses as being afflicted with delayed adolescence, and attacking the journalists who defended freedom of thought and expression in the press and on TV. To cap it all off, he'd quoted three lines of verse; you could almost hear him saying, *Look, Mom! Look, Dad! Look how smart I am. I can memorize poetry!*

Nothing remains of antiquity's virtues,
for when virtue perishes, so nations must too

If a nation's morals are wounded, then weep, for the wound is fatal

To better yourself, make morals your guide
For only through morals are the sinful set right.

But the flag still flew. In the furor surrounding my imprisonment, a number of parliamentarians who'd come from literary or intellectual backgrounds began a campaign to change the public decency law and put an end to the use of custodial sentences for crimes of opinion, which contravened the new constitution. Two members of parliament, Nadia Henry and Ahmad Sa'id, each presented a proposal for a change in the law, and many of my friends and other politicians worked hard—harder than anyone could have expected—behind the scenes to make it happen.

On hot nights in prison when I couldn't get to sleep, and when finally a cool breeze crept through the window before dawn, I fantasized that these efforts would pay off. Imagine if the law were to change, and I were to get out of prison as a result! It would be a victory that would bring meaning to every one of those sleepless nights, and that would save others from having to go through the same thing.

The bill was put before the legislation committee, and although it was supported by more than 160 parliamentarians, the representative of the Ministry of Justice objected on the grounds that it fell within the remit of his ministry, who he said were already working on a full overhaul of the law that would remove all the articles concerning custodial sentences for cases of freedom of opinion and expression. After the ministry spokesperson said this, certain parliamentarians changed their minds for no apparent reason. One particular member started attacking the proposal and even calling for Naguib Mahfouz to be posthumously brought to justice because he had offended public decency and his works had incited degeneracy and vice. This was the bizarre and arbitrary way things played out in Egypt.

A couple of months later, the president was inaugurating one of his grand national projects—some fish farm or sewage plant, who knows—when a member of parliament asked to speak, and requested that the government postpone its decision to raise gasoline prices. The president got mad at this and responded derisively with a famous line from a TV comedy. The cameras zoomed in on the parliamentarian right as the president was making fun of him, and showed his face going from deep tomato to sickly yellow. I think the guy must have wet his pants; he was trembling like a frightened kitten. Fate's little jokes: it was the same guy who'd opposed the amendments to the law and flexed his idiot muscles by attacking a dead Nobel Prize–winning author.

Day 161: Saturday, July 30, 2016

"Offensive" is frequently but a synonym for "unusual"; and a great work of art is of course always original, and thus by its very nature should come as a more or less shocking surprise.

 —Vladimir Nabokov

WHERE'S THE EVIDENCE?

THE RULING DIDN'T ACTUALLY SAY which phrases I'd been sent to prison for. Which were the words that had offended public modesty? Which were the sentences I had deployed to incite vice and depravity and strike at the very foundations of society? In seven pages of A3 paper, covering more than a few lessons in literature and rhetoric, there was no sign of my own words anywhere.

Court rulings were required to state clearly the evidence on which they were based. If you'd committed a murder, there had to be a murder weapon. I'd supposedly committed obscenity, but what with?

Since the ruling didn't deign to mention the offending expressions, I was left—violator of public morals though I was—not knowing what I'd actually done. And I wasn't the only one: the rest of society didn't know either. (Surely that was a dangerous thing—those words were still at large, lurking in dictionaries and encyclopedias, and at any moment they might slip off the page and out into society, where they could do unimaginable harm!) How, then, could other writers make sure they didn't make the same mistake, if they didn't know exactly which words were liable to land them in prison?

The court was all-powerful, and nobody in the country had any right to object to its rulings. But it still couldn't mention those unmentionable words I'd written; somehow, they overpowered the court, splattering muck on its robes and poking fun at its sacrosanct authority. There were words that the highest power in the land didn't dare to utter, or even to list as criminal—secret, terrible words that left people's lips only in times of anger, or when fucking, or joking, or fighting. And the thing is, when it came down to it, the court ruling was irrelevant. There was no way they could stop me from using these vile, offensive, harmful, angry expressions. I was a writer. Why would I ever give up such a terrific, untouchable power, capable of destroying society and its values? Why would I stop playing with such a magnificent toy?

Day 179: Wednesday, August 17, 2016

Dreamed I was at Amr El-Kafrawi and Marwa's house. They had a beautiful painting on the wall that they told me was by the Qalini sisters. I asked the two sisters if I could interview them and proposed an open conversation that would take place over the course of a day spent together.

I was sitting in their car. It stopped somewhere between Minyat Sandub—where I was born—and Sandub. Suddenly one of the sisters fainted, and, as if it were a perfectly ordinary thing, I picked her up and began carrying her through thick fog toward another car. Suddenly I made out the figure of Tarek el-Ariss waving happily at me through the fog. I couldn't wave back, because my arms were full of the unconscious artist, so instead I shouted out something that, as it left my lips, seemed both magical and pleasurable. "On the foggy path," I called out to him. "On the foggy path!"

Day 185: Tuesday, August 23, 2016

I'm getting good at interpreting dreams and reading coffee grounds. I can see how people here get so obsessed with dreams and visions.

Everybody thinks they've been wronged; everybody's a victim of some grave injustice, usually by way of a woman's vengeance or unbridled state power. But the story of the prophet Yusuf sustains them with the hope that one day they'll be free and win back their rights and the rights of their children. Amid misery, despair, and humiliation, only dreams are capable of inspiring hope. Yusuf prophesied the fate of his companions in prison, and while everybody here dreams, and hurries to share their dreams with those around them, the role of Yusuf suits me because it means I can sit and listen, then use the language I have to give them hope.

This newfound role came about of its own accord. A cell-mate told me about a dream he'd had, and I combined what little I knew of psychoanalysis with the information I had about the man and his case, and came up with a few sentences, which I uttered as I looked him directly in the eye. I kept it vague and imprecise, as open to interpretation as a line of prose poetry. Two days later, the man was back.

"Mr. Naji," he said admiringly, "God's definitely given you something." He told me that what I'd said had come true: his daughter had gotten a new job. And so my reputation as a dream interpreter was made.

Somewhere along the way, I added in coffee grounds for fun. I set 8:00 p.m., right after dinner, as the appointed time. I don't read more than two cups in one night. The important thing is the ritual. We pour the coffee as we talk, then I ask my client to say "Bismillah" and drink the coffee in three sips. I place a saucer over the cup and flip it over. There's a minute of silence, then I pick up the cup and begin to explain.

"We're going to divide the cup into quarters. The first quarter, bottom right, tells us about your material situation; the next, above it, tells us about the person you love and your family; the third quarter concerns the future; and the fourth concerns your friends and enemies. And now we'll read the spectral shapes formed by the coffee grounds, and listen to what the cup is trying to whisper..."

ONE MORNING IN SINAI

WE'D ARRIVED IN SINAI THE day before. It was April 2015. The sea and sky were blue; the mountains were at our backs. I was exhausted and dispirited, broken and unhealed after a string of failed romances. My life felt like something floating in a stagnant green pond. But now I was finally at the Red Sea and looking forward to seeing the colorful fish and corals. I had put my goggles on and was heading for the water when my cell phone rang. It was the office of *Literature Review* calling to say they'd received a summons from the public prosecutor addressed to me and Tarek al-Taher, who was the editor in chief. Sadness crawled over me. I felt it kneeling on my chest to bully me into leaving the magic of Sinai and my friends, after months of waiting for a vacation.

On the bus back to Cairo, I thought about how everything had started, and tried to work out where the blow had come from. I began working at *Literature Review* as an intern when I was eighteen, and continued working for the magazine after high school graduation. By 2015, I had covered the arts and culture scene in the Middle East for more than ten years. *Literature Review* was founded in 1993 as a weekly magazine focusing on the literary world, with the goal of providing in-depth coverage of cultural, political, and social issues. It was distributed across the Arabic-speaking region.

During the year the Muslim Brotherhood was in power, our then editor in chief, 'Abla al-Ruwayni, stepped aside and we were sent a replacement we didn't know. He just flew in one day from the Sultanate of Oman wearing a suit and waistcoat and smoking cheap cigarettes that he kept in a showy metal case. He even used a plastic cigarette holder. Ever since it was founded by the late Gamal al-Ghitani, *Literature Review* had been run collaboratively by the editor in chief and an editorial board composed of former editors. Al-Ghitani often used to hand over the editorship of individual issues to colleagues, especially if it was a themed issue focusing on a topic of their interest or expertise.

The editorial board tried as best they could to work with the new editor from Oman. But nothing turned out right; the results were literary crap and miserable office politics. We ended up dividing the magazine between the conflicting parties—him and us—which brought about a bizarre state of affairs in which the editorial section would heap praise on the Brotherhood's cultural policies, while the rest of the issue criticized them roundly.

Things ultimately reached a breaking point. Most of the staff writers went on strike, and for months the new editor put out the magazine by himself, with the help of a small faction of the staff. They produced masterpieces like an issue with the beaming face of Islamist leader Khairat el-Shater on the cover, accompanied by the headline HAS THIS MAN SAVED EGYPTIAN CULTURE?

The editor, who referred to himself as "Doctor," became the butt of several disparaging jokes online and in the arts scene. One satirized his insistence that Karl Marx had converted to Islam at the end of his life; the guy would actually make up little maxims praising Islam and the Prophet, peace be upon him, and attribute them to Marx. I never had the faintest idea why he did this. Was it a genuine attempt to win over left-leaning readers and put them back on the true path by convincing them to join the Brotherhood?

Surprisingly, his eccentric presence didn't come to an end with the eclipse of Brotherhood rule. June 30, 2013, came and went, and his name was still there as editor in chief. But, this being the age of coups d'état, my colleagues quickly got things under control. The editorial board took over, and we brought out the next issue ourselves, while he hid out of sight in his office. Occasionally he was permitted to write his weekly column, and it goes without saying that following the events of June 30, his articles went instantly from kissing the Brotherhood's ass to kissing the ass of the military government, which had just disposed of them. This strange situation lasted a whole year, until the board of our parent company, Akhbar al-Yawm, got a new chair, and Tarek al-Taher was appointed as our new editor in chief. The Doctor's reign was finally over—though this didn't stop him from appearing on TV and introducing himself as *"Literature Review*'s legitimate editor in chief" for months afterward.

The media underwent some pretty rapid changes during the years that we were embroiled in these conflicts over editorship and management, and since it was published by a state-owned press, *Literature Review* was ultimately hamstrung. We couldn't set up a basic website to archive our publications, because we had to do what Akhbar al-Yawm told us to do. We sold many more copies abroad than within Egypt, and there were whole regions of the country where the magazine wasn't available. We wanted to improve our distribution system, but we couldn't touch it, because it was all in the hands of Akhbar al-Yawm. The company was bloated, unimaginative, and bureaucratic. The stranglehold of state employees had turned it into an open grave where the corpses of once-vibrant publications rotted in the sun and were feasted on by parasitic advertising reps. But still we resisted, because there was nothing else we could do.

Around that time, Mohamed Shoair, one of the most talented journalists and writers I've worked with and learned from, became editorial director of the review, and we started work on an issue themed around Downtown Cairo—the center of the modern city and the beating heart of its literature and arts scene. I'd just turned in my second novel, *Using Life*, and was looking forward to seeing it published. The city of Cairo is the axis of its plot, and numerous key events in the novel take place in Downtown, so Shoair asked if the magazine could print an excerpt in the special issue. I scrolled through the final draft looking for a chapter that was set in Downtown and roughly met the word count he'd asked for. I settled on chapter five, put it in an email to him, and hit SEND.

The issue, including my piece, appeared while I was on a work trip to Berlin. I didn't have much internet access, so I wasn't following the news, but shortly before I was due to fly home, I got a message from my friend Ahmed Wael telling me something was up. When I arrived in Cairo I went straight to the office, only to find the place in a state of high anxiety. Apparently the disgruntled former editor had bought a huge number of copies, photocopied the pages containing my contribution, and taken them to Akhbar al-Yawm, where he'd handed them out to every employee he could find, screeching dramatically as he did so: "Look what's happened to *Literature Review* since I left! It's been taken over by commies and they're promoting sex and atheism!"

He was attempting to get the staff riled up against the magazine and against the journalists who'd recently assumed leadership at the company. And from what I was told by al-Taher and Shoair, it sounded like it had worked, because the new chairman of the board of Akhbar al-Yawm was spooked and felt like he had to do something to save face in front of his outraged employees. So he decided to suspend me with pay for a month.

I was furious at the injustice of it, especially since there'd been no disciplinary hearing, as our regulations stipulated there had to be. Al-Taher and Shoair appeared to be observing a truce with the board, which everybody thought was a sensible course of action, given the situation the magazine was in, so they told me to relax and consider it an extra-long paid holiday.

I was at home a few days later when a letter arrived at the door by tracked delivery. It was from Akhbar al-Yawm, officially notifying me of my suspension, which it said was in response to my having "violated the journalistic code of conduct." This was in August 2014, and the novel wasn't yet out. My fears seemed to be confirmed when a journalist from another paper called me up asking if it was true that I'd been banned from writing. I said no, and didn't give any comment, and he didn't end up publishing anything. Some of my friends thought I was making a mistake by keeping silent, but the way I saw it, a media frenzy would affect how the book was received when it came out, pushing it into the realm of gossip and scandal rather than into the literary world, where it belonged. There was also my affection and respect for my colleagues at *Literature Review*, who thought that escalating the conflict wouldn't help our attempts to save the beleaguered magazine.

The matter was soon forgotten, and I enjoyed my unofficial holiday. But when I went back to work, I found that my relationship with the magazine had soured. A cloud of anger hung over my head whenever I entered the Akhbar al-Yawm building, and I was gripped with nihilism. What was I even doing here?

It wasn't like I was doing it for the money; our paltry salaries were nowhere close to keeping up with inflation and rising prices. This was a problem all state-employed journalists had to contend with, and it wasn't new, of course: I'd been earning most of my income from freelance writing and other gigs for years by then. I'd simply stayed loyal to *Literature Review* out of a profound sense of admiration for and goodwill toward one of the very few publications that stood for absolute freedom of opinion and expression and didn't waver even in times of crisis, like during the *Banquet for Seaweed* controversy. And now I'd been disciplined for violating the journalists' code of conduct by exercising that very right, and had not even been given the chance to defend myself.

I was glad when the novel came out. I felt like I'd finally achieved something after four years of floundering in a murky sea, dealing with mistakes that couldn't be fixed and painful losses of things I'd thought I possessed. At the book launch at Gallery Medrar, there was an exhibition of Ayman al-Zorkany's illustrations from the novel, and a short cartoon film of one of the chapters was shown. I was pleased I'd managed to do things my own way, and happy my friends were there, as joyful in my presence as I was in theirs, and excited we could share this happy moment and our love of literature and of one another.

Day 44: Monday, April 4, 2016

I dreamed that as a result of climate change, a new species of talking bear had appeared. The bears had begun to migrate outside their original environment and demand their rights, and of course they were treated like illegal immigrants. Even though they could talk, they weren't treated as beings fully endowed with reason and will. Laws were issued banning the marriage of male bears with human females. Then a sex tape was leaked online, showing a BDSM encounter between a bear and a woman, and the world was immediately swept up in controversy and violence. Amid this uproar, I set out on a long journey and finally arrived at a breathtakingly beautiful beach, isolated and calm, where I met my sister and nephew, and we swam happily together in the sea.

Today an elderly prisoner fainted and fell straight to the floor. He's a huge, sturdy man, and it took six people to pick him up. His bunk neighbor ran over with a strip of pills and stuck one under his tongue. It turns out he has a heart problem, and in the poorly ventilated cell he regularly has these episodes. We called the guard, who called the doctor, and finally they opened the cell and took him to the clinic.

Day 50: Sunday, April 10, 2016

The thunder and lightning and rain continued all night. Couldn't sleep. Then the guys in the next cell over started screaming and banging on the metal door. It went on for two whole hours. "Sergeant!" they yelled, again and again. "Sergeant, he's dying!"

THE COURT AND
THE MORGUE

BACK IN NIGHTMARISH CAIRO, I MET with Mahmoud Othman, a lawyer from the Association for Freedom of Thought and Expression, and my own lawyer Nasir Amin, and we headed to the public prosecutor's office, which had its headquarters in Zeinhum court. With us were al-Taher, who was facing the charges with me; a lawyer from the Journalists' Union; and another from Akhbar al-Yawm. This last guy shook my hand with obvious distaste in front of the court building, and as we made our way inside to the busy elevators, I could hear him muttering something to the effect that we shouldn't have been publishing such "filth" anyway.

Zeinhum court sat at the end of Bayram al-Tunisi Street, a long, narrow road that sliced through the archaeological remains of Old Cairo and the working-class neighborhood of Sayyida Zeinab. Next to the court was an animal hospital run by a charity and Zeinhum morgue, or the Forensic Medicine Authority. The court itself was a modern neoclassical thing, whose enormous white columns had long ago turned the dusty yellow so characteristic of Cairo; in front of it, a high wall partially blocked the view of the cemeteries and ruins of the old city.

We'd agreed that al-Taher would go in first with the lawyers to meet the prosecuting attorney. They'd see how it went and pick a strategy accordingly. If it looked like there was some room for discussion, they'd call me to come and join them in the interview. If not, they'd claim I just hadn't shown up. You never knew; the public prosecution might do something unexpected—like decide to hold me in custody until the trial.

Outside in the corridor I took in the miserable atmosphere. The whole place smelled rotten. Families were camped out on the floor. Handcuffed detainees sat in the stairwells smoking, waiting to be taken before the prosecutor; children griped in the arms of elderly women whose black abayas trailed in the dust. Suddenly and without warning, everything would pause. Two police officers would appear—one plainclothes, one in uniform—and sweep through the crowds, bellowing to those standing to step aside and to those sitting on the floor to stand up, to make way for his Honor the judge. Then, preceded by a potent waft of cologne to shield him against the rancid odor of the courthouse air, his Honor would appear briefly before his subjects, striding quickly and purposefully to make sure his gaze didn't fall on any of the people who were frozen to the spot until he had passed, leaving the thick scent of his cologne clinging to the walls behind him.

That was my first encounter with the grandeur of the power of the criminal justice system. I'd known the power of the police, which was like the power of street dogs: they sure made a terrifying noise, but if you could keep your nerve, they'd get out of your way. I'd known the power of the men of religion, which came with expansive smiles and advice, and an assault of crazed love that willed you to be what it wanted—and if you tried to run or refuse, it would slaughter you with that same crazed emotion. Thanks to Tahrir Square and the neighborhoods of 'Abdin and Bulaq Abu al-'Ila, I'd also known the power of weapons, the armored vehicles that occupy the streets, so you have no choice but to turn back. Even when you think they will protect you, they won't hesitate to run you over. And I'd also known the power of a man with money and his associates and his fleas who suck your blood and sap your strength; the power, too, of the masses, of the mob, of tramps and vermin, of rodents and hoofed beasts.

But I had never witnessed the power of the judge. He needed no additional tools to enact its sovereignty: he simply spoke, and was. Rather like God created the world with a command of two letters—*Be!*— so the judge could speak and know he would be obeyed. Even if you killed him or fled, his rulings would still be engraved upon your history. The scope of his author-ity extended into the future. And where God would forgive, repentance offered no protection against the power of the judge.

Absorbed in the dramatization of justice taking place around me, I watched until the pace of movement gradually slowed and the employees began to leave for the day. It was nearly 5:00 p.m. and al-Taher was still in the interview. The prosecutor had questioned him aggressively, according to one of our lawyers, who later shared with me some of the more absurd moments of the interview. Apparently the prosecutor had threatened to charge me with drug offenses because the protagonist of *Using Life*, Bassam Bahgat, smokes a spliff in the section excerpted in the magazine, and since the novel is narrated in the first person, this amounted in his view to a confession that I smoked hash and had sex.

The lawyer from Akhbar al-Yawm came out glowering. "Who is this Lady Spoon, anyway—a friend of yours?" he asked me sternly, referring to a character in the book in whom the prosecution attorney had shown a great interest. I fought back the urge to snort at his stupidity. Things were serious, and a thoughtless reaction could have consequences. The legal team thought I should leave; they said there was no point getting embroiled in an interview with this prosecutor. He was a lost cause. One of our attorneys spent half an hour explaining the difference between fiction and nonfiction to him. He insisted that the text before him was a confession to debauchery and narcotics use, and that it promoted illicit sexual relations—and if it wasn't true, then it was still a crime to have published it, because we were disseminating false or misleading information. At this point al-Taher attempted to draw an analogy to a TV series starring Ghada Abdel Razek: "Surely you couldn't try the actress for murder," he reasoned, "just because she'd killed someone in one of the episodes?" The prosecutor took in this new piece of information and snapped, dead serious: "So you're telling me this is a TV show now?" Al-Taher tried to explain, but the prosecutor was warming to his theme. "In that case," he replied with a confident flourish, "where are the other episodes?"

The bit I liked best was when al-Taher got so frustrated with how long the interrogation was taking that he delivered an eloquent speech on the role of the judiciary and the public prosecutor's office in defending cultural enlightenment and the values of freedom of conscience and expression, citing the commendable stance of Justice Muhammad Nur, the prosecutor who, in a well-known case from 1927, had investigated the literary giant Taha Hussein for allegedly insulting Islam in his scholarship on pre-Islamic poetry. Muhammad Nur, said Tarek, had upheld freedom of speech by closing the case against Hussein, but here the prosecutor stopped him. "Justice Muhammad Nur?" he said authoritatively. "I don't know anyone by that name."

In the end, the questioning went on until six in the evening, and there was even some talk of transferring al-Taher to the precinct where the original case had been brought, before releasing him from there, but finally they let him go. After that experience, our legal team decided not to respond to any further summonses, a strategy that they thought would force the public prosecution to either drop the case—as often happened with

cases brought by private individuals of no particular impor-
tance—or to decide that as upholders of the law and protectors
of public morality, they had to bring the case to court. We also
decided to keep quiet. If we escalated the issue and made a
fuss in the media, it might provoke them more, but if we said
nothing, maybe they'd forget about the whole thing.

Here it's worth mentioning what was going on at the time
in Egypt more broadly. The new constitution adopted in 2014
contained numerous articles guaranteeing freedom of conscience
and expression and banning the use of detention in freedom-
of-speech cases. For the cultural and media elites this was the
victory they had secured through their support for their "revolution" of June 30, 2013. The judiciary, on the other hand, was
furious about this new limitation on its powers and determined
to bring journalists to heel. And so the public prosecutor's
office began deliberately detaining journalists on charges relat-
ing to their political opinions and professional activities. The
Journalists' Union took the issue to the Administrative Court,
which ruled that it was unconstitutional to detain journalists,
but the public prosecutor's office wouldn't budge. Not only did
they go ahead with the new cases, they also decided to reopen
all pending cases involving charges against journalists. One of
those cases was mine.

By the summer of 2015, there were twenty-two members of
the Journalists' Union imprisoned on cases related to freedom of
expression and opinion, and God knows how many others that
didn't have any links to the union. The union was at loggerheads

with the public prosecutor, and the arrests of journalists continued apace, with more and more detained, awaiting trial on charges that were pure fantasy.

The situation exploded with the Tiran and Sanafir protests in April 2016, which broke out when the Egyptian government ceded sovereignty over two strategically significant Red Sea islands to Saudi Arabia, provoking popular fury. Security forces stormed the Journalists' Union building and arrested journalists 'Amr Badr and Mahmud al-Saqa, in clear contravention of the laws regarding the union and the inviolability of its headquarters, and the public prosecutor's office released an unprecedented statement, essentially saying it was very happy with its own work, thank you very much, and would continue chasing journalists wherever they went.

The union and the journalists themselves weren't able to oppose the public prosecution office, so instead they directed their anger at the minister of the interior. In response, the public prosecutor charged the president of the union and two executive committee members with harboring criminal suspects. Those criminals were Badr and al-Saqa, who were accused of publishing "false news" by claiming that the two islands, Tiran and Sanafir, belonged to Egypt, not Saudi Arabia. Then, in a collaborative move by the public prosecution office, the security apparatus, and government informers inside the union, a final blow was struck against the union's executive committee, who had led the peaceful opposition to the public prosecutor's tyrannical overreach, when union president Yahya Qullash and his supporters were ousted in the internal elections of 2017.

But let's go back to the summer of 2015 for a moment. I had gone on another vacation to Sinai, twelve weeks after our first visit to the prosecuting attorney. This time, I'd brought Yasmine—it was her first time visiting Taba and Nuwayba', two of my favorite places in the world—and the weather was gorgeous, the sea was clear, and we had the campsite more or less to ourselves. We slept under the stars and built castles of dreams. I was engulfed in my love for her. The past couldn't reach us here; I wanted to run away with her into the future. Then, a few days after our return to Cairo, I awoke to a string of missed calls from a number I didn't recognize, and when I finally picked up, it was a fellow journalist asking for a comment on the fact that my case was going to trial. "Trial?" I asked. "What trial?" What the hell was he talking about and where had he gotten this information? He said it had come directly from the prosecutor for Bulaq district, who had taken the unusual step of releasing the decision to the media.

"So what's your comment?" he asked. I declined to respond and hung up. I needed to talk to my lawyers first. I crawled out of bed and staggered into the bathroom to wash my face and brush my teeth, then went into the living room and threw myself onto the couch.

Day 29: Sunday, March 20, 2016

Dreamed I was imprisoned in a dark room, waiting for someone. I waited and waited, then opened the door to find an old man raping a child while rats swarmed around them. I realized then that I was having a nightmare, and tried to wake up, but I couldn't move, and the old man who was controlling the nightmare was attempting to make me have sex with an enormous rat the size of an infant. I leaped up, screaming. I opened my eyes; I was in the darkness of the cell.

ENLIGHTENMENT

WAEL ABD EL-FATTAH LENT US the space belonging to his web magazine, *Madina*, in Zamalek, for a meeting with friends and colleagues. I was overjoyed to have them around me. It felt like I wasn't alone in the trial: these were my partners in crime.

The aim of the meeting was ostensibly to talk to the lawyers Nasir Amin and Mahmoud Othman and decide on a strategy for the defense, but since the public prosecution office had leaked the news, and along with it a copy of the decision to refer to trial, we were now also embroiled in a media battle that we needed to manage as carefully as the legal battle.

With me that day were journalists, film directors, writers, people who worked in advertising and the media, producers, graphic designers, artists, software developers, and unemployed people—but first and foremost, they were the people I loved.

My gang. I didn't feel I owed them anything, because there's no room for transactions between friends.

This circle of people was getting wider by the day. I regularly received messages of solidarity out of the blue. Nasir decided we should choose three well-known names from among my many supporters, who could be witnesses for the defense, which is why we settled on Gaber 'Asfur, Muhammad Salmawi, and Sonallah Ibrahim. Even though only one of them, Salmawi, knew me personally, they immediately agreed, saying they were glad to help out however they could.

One of the most surprising experiences for me was our meeting with 'Asfur in his home in Dokki. I'd gone to thank him for his support, and Rashid, a filmmaker and friend, had come with me to record a short clip of him talking about the case. After we switched off the camera, 'Asfur turned to me. "Listen, I support you one hundred percent," he said, "but let's talk about literature for a moment, not about the court case. Don't you think using that sort of language did the book a disservice and limited its chances of being read?"

"Sure," I replied, "but I didn't invent those words."

"Boy! Don't give me that. I know where the words come from. I've read the book, and I know you're trying to say that we've lost everything and are living in chaos. You want to paint a picture of what a mess the world is, and how corporations run our lives now. But why use those words when they might put the reader off and stop them from finishing the book or distract them from your message?"

I paused for a moment, trying to accept his logic, but I couldn't. I shook my head. "No, I don't really see it that way, Dr. 'Asfur."

"Take Naguib Mahfouz, for example," he said. "He wrote whatever he wanted, but he did it in simple, clear language that reached everybody and didn't put them off."

"Yes, and he still ended up getting stabbed in the neck," I protested.

"But his legacy is still with us. His influence continues to this day. Look, bear with me here—I'm an old-fashioned type, I know, and I believe literature brings enlightenment. You've printed, what, a thousand copies of your novel? Now, just imagine you'd written the same fantastic novel but without using that language—think how much more widely it would be read and how much more influential it would be."

"Okay, imagine I did that, Dr. 'Asfur. Let's say the novel is read by a million people, or let's say it magically ends up being read by all ninety million Egyptians. What would happen then? What would change, exactly? Do people automatically become enlightened by reading novels? And what would I stand to gain?"

"But don't you want to be well known? Don't you want your book to be read by as many people as possible?"

"I'm from the internet generation, Doctor. If I wanted that sort of thing, I could post naked photos of myself online, and by tomorrow I'd be more famous than Naguib Mahfouz ever was. But I didn't spend five years writing a novel because I want to be famous. If anything, my journalism satisfies that desire."

"But writing only comes alive through people. You know, it makes me sad that my children and grandchildren don't read Naguib Mahfouz."

This debate went on for more than an hour, and it was one of the oddest conversations about the book I'd ever had. I understood what he was saying, and he what I was saying, but it was like there was a pane of glass between us obstructing any real communication. I couldn't really explain what I meant, and he just kept repeating, "Forgive me, I'm an old man, and I believe in enlightenment." I just couldn't fathom the logic of this "enlightenment."

At one point we got into a detailed discussion of the language I'd used in the novel, and 'Asfur made a surprising observation about my use of certain foreign words. I was rather embarrassed by how closely and attentively he'd read the novel. It would have been enough for him to have said he believed unconditionally in freedom of opinion and expression, but he'd really given the book some thought, and in fact wrote a long review in *al-Ahram* before the trial. I was amazed by the liveliness of his mind and his ability to follow and scrutinize the literary scene with a clear-sightedness that I didn't have a quarter of.

Over the course of my journalism and writing career, I'd repeatedly attacked all three of them—'Asfur himself, Ibrahim, and Salmawi. I'd made fun of what I called "Ibrahim's Coca-Cola phobia," an obsessive anti-imperialism that dominated most of his oeuvre, and I'd repeatedly criticized 'Asfur's and Salmawi's political stances. But now the warmth, affection, courage, and commitment they showed were changing my views.

During this period, before I went to prison, I never asked myself any existential questions about the meaning and purpose of my life. I wasn't brave enough to think of myself as a writer. I had close friends and colleagues who didn't even know I wrote literature, and I continued to introduce myself as a journalist, like my ID card said. But as my legal crisis deepened, I could see that the journalism crowd was drifting away—they felt strange and distant to me, and no doubt I seemed the same to them—while the literature people extended their hands to strengthen me and lift me up.

In front of the courthouse at al-Gala', I stood with Yasmine waiting for the three men to arrive. It was the first day of the trial. Salmawi arrived first, smiling broadly as he got out of the car. He saw I was anxious and started cracking jokes to lighten the mood, his expansive, charismatic personality making everyone comfortable as usual. I was keeping my eyes peeled for Ibrahim, who I knew was on his way, and spotted him looking for the entrance. I called out to him and we shook hands. Then he greeted Salmawi and the pair went into the court building with Yasmine, while I headed to a nearby café with friends to wait for news.

The prosecutor took the court by surprise with an eccentric speech in which he attempted to show off everything he'd memorized at school while attacking my character with some unique metaphors (apparently I was "a yellow viper curled around the necks of the children and youth of the nation"). Amin presented his defense and called Sonallah Ibrahim to the stand to refute the accusations that the novel was "pornographic" and establish that it was a work of literature. The prosecutor got angrier and angrier and started challenging Ibrahim to read the passage in question out loud. Ibrahim ignored him, but the man wouldn't drop it. "Could you read it out loud?" he screamed. "Could you?" Finally Ibrahim lost his temper and held out a hand to take the book, planning to go ahead and read it out loud, but Nasir stopped him, objecting that it wasn't pertinent to the case. Muhammad Salmawi took the stand, too, and although 'Asfur turned up after the judge had already retired to deliberate, when the judge was informed of his arrival he summoned him to his office.

Nasir and Mahmoud Othman came out of the hearing feeling optimistic. We assumed I'd be convicted, but the fact that the judge had listened to the testimonies and the defense arguments in full suggested he might be planning to issue a guilty verdict without any real punishment. In the history of Egypt's modern legal system, no one had ever been sent to prison under article 178 of the penal code. Usually they just got a slap on the wrist—a fine or a suspended sentence. In 2010, I'd attended the trial of Magdy El Shafee, a writer and artist who'd been convicted of obscenity under the same article, for a strip of his cartoon *Metro*. It ended in a guilty verdict, with a fine of five thousand Egyptian pounds for both him and his publisher. That was the worst-case scenario for us, we thought.

There was certainly no point hoping for an innocent verdict, but at least we'd tried to use the trial as an opportunity to draw attention to article 178 and other articles that prescribed custodial sentences in crimes of freedom of opinion and expression. We'd argued that they contravened the new constitution and should be struck down, and the use of custodial sentences ended. Amin was genuinely hopeful that by arguing that the article was unconstitutional, he'd get the judge to refer the case to the constitutional court, and then maybe we really would have a chance of achieving our goal. We waited and hoped, until finally the verdict was issued on January 2, 2016.

"Innocent."

"What?!"

"I know, that's what I said. But it's innocent."

"Oh my god. Thank you, Mahmoud. Thank you so much."

After I ended the call I stood in a daze, unable to take in what I'd heard. I was so happy and so proud of my friends, my lawyers, and the brotherhood of writers who'd stood by my side. Back when everything kicked off, I'd just expected people to gossip about me; I'd never expected such enormous support from all those literary figures, many of whom I'd disagreed with and criticized.

For the rest of the day, I kept my head down, avoided phone calls, and said nothing to the press. But that evening, as I was heading out to a celebratory dinner with friends, my phone rang and I unthinkingly picked up, only to discover I was being broadcast live on Lamis Elhadidy's chat show. I was furious:

How had I ended up in this trap? Elhadidy gave a rambling introduction about how enlightened the judge in my case had proved himself to be, how he'd stood up for freedom of expression and the constitution, and then asked me a question that translated more or less as "Don't you agree, Ahmed? Come on, it's your turn to kiss ass now."

I hemmed and hawed for a few seconds, then said that the verdict was a message to the public prosecutor's office that they should stick to their job—safeguarding the constitution, the rule of law, and the rights of citizens—rather than setting themselves up as crusaders for public morality who instructed the population as to what they should and shouldn't do.

"Yes, yes, thank you very much," said Elhadidy hurriedly, then the line went dead.

Day 103: Thursday, June 2, 2016

Even my memories of sex are fading, and I've now failed twice to masturbate. No fantasies come to mind, and I have no urge to do it, but I have to so my sperm ducts don't get inflamed again.

Day 131: Thursday, June 30, 2016

In *Foucault's Pendulum*, Umberto Eco writes: "Once I know that I can remember whenever I like, I forget."

A fight broke out recently in the felons' cellblock, and as part of their punishment, they're now not allowed any sharp tools at all, including razor blades. Once a week, one of the intelligence guys comes in with an electric shaver, and the whole cellblock has a shave and "freshens up"—that is, trims their underarms and pubes—all with the same shaver. On the first Monday of the month, a barber comes in, again with a single shaver, to give everybody in the cell a matching buzz cut.

AN ABSENCE OF
CRIMINAL INTENT

A FEW WEEKS LATER, THE full innocent verdict was released, and it was the opposite of everything we had expected. We were amazed at how perceptive and intelligent it was.

> Whereas, regarding the merits of the claim, the Public Prosecutor referred both defendants to trial for offending public decency pursuant to Articles 178 and 200 bis (a)(2) of the Penal Code, which require the subjective criminal intent to offend public decency or to spread debauchery and vice, which is incompatible with the first defendant's act, namely the creation of a literary work that is the product of his imagination, and any phrases or expressions with which the Public Prosecutor found he had offended public decency appeared within the framework of literary writing and in the general

context of a fictional story, and likewise the sexual phrases and expressions contained within the literary work are an ordinary occurrence in many literary and poetic compositions, both historical and modern, as confirmed by the testimonies of Mr. Muhammad Salmawi and novelist Sonallah Ibrahim, who have satisfied the court that a literary work cannot be divorced from its context or examined piecemeal rather than as a whole. A literary work is a single creation which loses its integrity if a single piece is extracted from it.

The court also finds that in evaluating phrases and expressions that are offensive to public decency, it is difficult to arrive at any fixed measure thereof, for what a simple person might find offensive to decency is not perceived as such by an educated or specialized individual, and what an extremist finds offensive to decency is not perceived as such by an enlightened thinker.

The judge had found that there was no criminal intent.

The subject matter that arises in the field of medicine and scientific enquiry, for example, might appear offensive to non-specialists, but it is not offensive to doctors; the meaning lies in the attitude of the reader or viewer and their evaluation of the matter.

The expressions contained in the subject story which were viewed as offensive to public decency by the Public

Prosecutor are not considered by literary specialists or novelists to be offensive provided they occur within the context of an artistic literary work.

The measure thus differs from person to person according to culture, mindset, and education. The ideas and views espoused by scholars and intellectuals of past times were often the object of criticism and rejection by their own societies and yet are today recognized as scientific truths or creative masterpieces which enrich our society.

ANTI-MANIFESTO

ENDOWED WITH TONGUES OF FIRE, writers will defend themselves with every word they utter. But when they come before
the law, they are stripped of their power. They cannot use their
language, because that language is proof of their guilt. The
law itself is a highly coded language, and the right to use it is
granted only to those whose credentials permit them to enter
the palace of the law. Even if language is your bread and butter,
once inside the palace of the law, you'll need a translator. Your
translator is the attorney you hire to defend you.

As the writer attacks and parries, engaged in a fast-moving
and ever-changing court battle, even long-held convictions are
called into question. Without the critique of their peers and
the time to review and reconsider their work, a writer does
not grow and develop. Defending one's work over the course
of a trial becomes embarrassing. A year down the line—less,

even—you might find you've totally changed your mind about what you've written.

I've always found interviews with the media excruciating. Pressing me to explain my work, journalists seem to assume that writers understand the full dimensions of the writing process. They don't realize that writing is itself a way to understand, a way to doubt and question. Forced to defend myself, I always felt like the defense itself became a prison in which my relationship with literature was confined. I became trapped in a cage that they and I had constructed out of sex, obscenity, taboos, and my conflict with censorship.

How are you going to get out of this one, Ahmed? I asked myself. Do battles like this even come to an end, or are they just wars of attrition that drag on forever? And what about the third flower—where was I going to put the third flower?

Day 45: Tuesday, April 5, 2016

I've found a book. You have to shake it before you open it, because the letters blur and rearrange themselves whenever you close it, ink seeping through the pages to form new letters that in turn form new sentences. Shaking before opening fixes these new words and sentences into place. When you open the cover, you find an entirely new book. And once you've opened it, you have to read to the end—because if you close it, you'll never get another chance to finish it.

THE PATH
TO GREATNESS

OUR CELEBRATION OF THE INNOCENT verdict didn't last long. The law gives the prosecutor up to sixty days to appeal a judgment, and in less than one month, we received a summons from the appeals court.

In an appeals court, the defendant is required to attend in person, so unlike with the previous trial, I couldn't sit in a café somewhere nearby while the lawyers argued it out. Instead, I had to go to the court myself, hand over my ID, and be taken into the court's custody. But we were feeling optimistic: the worst-case scenario was that they'd find me guilty and issue a fine, so I showed up with a thick wad of cash in my pocket, ready to pay.

I appeared before a court consisting of three judges. My lawyers told me to stay silent; if asked a direct question by the judge, I was to respond in short answers they would whisper in my ears. At the actual appeal, the judge only asked me for my name and birth date. The only challenging part was suppressing my laughter as I listened to the prosecutor's speech, which described me as an evil snake spewing venom into the minds of Egypt's youth and children.

After the appeal trial, the sentence wasn't announced immediately; instead, my codefendant Tarek al-Taher and I were kept waiting in the courtroom until the day's hearings were finished. Finally, three police officers appeared and asked us to follow them. They led us through a maze of back corridors that were crowded with courthouse staff and prisoners, to an office where a young lieutenant sat at a battered desk with two other, higher-ranking police commanders. The lieutenant read out the sentence: two years for me, and a fine for al-Taher.

I burst out laughing, and al-Taher launched into a long, enraged monologue about how important he was and how it must all be a mistake. Ignoring him, the eldest and most senior of the three officers turned to me and asked what the offense was. I gave him the gist of it. Pointing one finger at me, the other fingers clutching a ritzy string of prayer beads, he said: "Listen, son. You're on the path to greatness now. I know that judge. He's a tough one and he makes some strange decisions. But you'll come out of this stronger. God is our sufficiency and the best of all providers! You've made a great man of yourself. Your name will go down in history."

"What am I meant to do with my greatness if I'm in prison?!" I spluttered, still laughing. "Can't you keep the greatness and leave me to play in the mud?"

Greatness. Eternity. Revelation. Enlightenment. Edification. Educating the people. Lighting the path. The superiority of the Islamic bidet over the achievements of Western culture. Authenticity and modernity. Why the Arabs have lagged while others have flourished. Self and other, East and West. Cairo the victorious, built by a lowly sweet-maker—I'd tried so hard to run away from all this. Toward what, I had no idea.

In prison, under the pressure to assimilate to my new social environment, I found myself on the receiving end of all kinds of unsolicited advice of this sort, which I nevertheless acknowledged with a nod, murmuring my assent in conversations like the one with the police commander, as I was told what to write about and how to write it. Everyone had an opinion, it turned out: army captains and criminals unanimously agreed that "the writer" has a "calling" and must be "the voice of the voiceless." You were burdened not only with writing about them and passing on their messages to others, but also with their instructions for how to go about it.

I got these petitions on a daily basis from my fellow convicted criminals, our companions in pretrial detention, and upstanding gentlemen of the Ministry of the Interior. One of them would spot me from a distance, come over, and say, "Hey, I've got a story for you. Good enough for TV, I swear." (The more educated ones would say, "You can use it for your next novel.") After I got to know them better, people would ask, when they noticed me sitting with pen and paper, "Are you writing about us? Are we going to be in your book?" Even outside prison, I've met people with the same strange desire to have their stories told, to have their lives written down or turned into a film or TV series. Both before prison and after, people have asked me, "Why don't you write about me?" I envy their confidence in themselves—and in my own humble self. How the hell are they so sure I'll write the story the way they want it? How can they entrust their deepest secrets and most meaningful experiences to someone they don't know, and authorize that person to release them into the wild?

People have their reasons. Some of them are trying to find out something the writer is concealing from them—how the writer sees them, what he or she thinks of them. What they really want is to look at themselves, so they make the writer a mirror; they want to see their experience and ingenuity represented in a grand and unique portrait. Then there are those with more conceited artistic pretensions who think their life stories are so full of exciting exploits that other people will find them entertaining: readers will marvel, they're convinced, at the richness and drama of their experiences, and of course the intelligence and tenacity of the main character. The dumbest reason of all comes courtesy of those who think the writer will turn their life into a smash TV show and make them famous or—worse—rich.

Writers have their own motivations for telling people's stories, but as prison writing goes to show, they don't always make for great literature. Writing about prison means writing about other prisoners, and more often than not, it becomes an anthropological exercise in which the writer encounters representatives of unfamiliar social classes and professions, the legal and the less legal, and is so exhilarated by their discoveries that they forget what it was they originally wanted to say. With this kind of writing it often feels to me like the writer has filtered out their own personal experience and instead decided to entertain their readers with a cast of characters that are ultimately dramatic, not human—and don't even get me started on the way political prison writers instrumentalize the stories of other prisoners.

I couldn't maintain that kind of barrier between myself and my cellmates. Some became friends. Their stories weren't theater; their lives weren't newsworthy. Sometimes they shared secrets and showed me photos of their families and children. I've now lost track of some of them, and I wonder if they're still in prison. Some of them got out and cut their ties with that world; others send me messages from time to time. But even when the people themselves are lost to memory, I don't find myself compelled to exploit their stories or make an exhibit out of them. If I overcome my reservations and do try to write about someone, a question bobs to the surface of my consciousness like a red egg in a sea of milk: Do I have the right to violate that person's privacy? Is it a good enough excuse to say I'm documenting that person's experience or seeking to understand it?

If you're writing for history's sake, it doesn't stop there. With their sights set on posterity, these prison writers think of their work as testimony. They describe each person they've met in painstaking detail, but once the book is out, some former cellmate will come along and decide it's fake or defamatory and write their own offering to posterity. Competing testimonies multiply, each claiming to be the authority on history.

But if you're a writer who doesn't give a fuck about history, a single meal shared with twenty men around tin trays balanced on a box of trash counts as bread and salt: a relationship of obligation that demands you write about the frustration and humiliation of prison without reducing its victims and their secrets to figures of drama or entertainment.

Day 24: Tuesday, March 15, 2016

I feel like I'm stuck with a bunch of middle school students who're just discovering their sexual organs. Anytime a group of males get together, they develop their annoying in-jokes, so imagine how much worse it is when they're living in one another's pockets 24-7. Words get completely evacuated of their meaning, so only their sexual connotations are left.

Someone will say something like "It's behind you," and half the men in the cell will snicker. Then someone will reply, "Hey, watch out back there!," and the other half will burst out laughing. My balls cringe inside my scrotum. Anything involving "underneath," "on top," "behind," "giving" or "taking" something, or "putting it in" is fair game for their innuendo.

Most of these men have gray hair. But they're so far removed now from their social status, family roles, and professional or socioeconomic positions, and so far out of sight of the watchful eyes of society, that they regress to their teenage years and turn into boys who love X-rated humor.

"Frankly, the only thing that irritates me these days is imitation, even when it is very old, and what I truly hope for from the generation that will come after us, the generation that could take us to a global level, is that they be more faithful in this respect. Faithful to themselves."

—Gamal al-Ghitani, *Naguib Mahfouz Remembers*

Day 40: Thursday, March 31, 2016

Found a copy of Naguib Mahfouz's *Adrift on the Nile* in the library. I can't have been older than thirteen when I read it for the first time; back then, I'd found it in the school library. Re-reading it today, I thought it was excellent. Every sentence has its own meaning; the book's depth comes from its scattered-ness and absurdity. And unlike the first time I read it, I wasn't annoyed by its theatricality. The only thing that annoyed me was finding a page missing from the middle of the book, and then when I found another six torn out later, I lost my shit. That's the lowest of the low. You can burn books, put their authors in prison, ban them, or confiscate them. But tearing pages out is a punishment so nasty no one's thought of it yet. Then, on the last page, I found a handwritten note: "This book is good but contains blasphemous and obscene material. The reader should pray for God's forgiveness after reading." I'm guessing its author was the person who tore out the offending pages, in the hope of saving his fellow prisoners from sin.

OBSCENITY

I do not think that obscenity necessarily should be limited to exciting sexual feeling. I can understand people reading something that does not excite them in such a manner but which they might still pass on as being obscene. I should say a thing is obscene by the ordinary language used and by what it does to the average reader. It need not necessarily be what the author intended. On these grounds, I think there are ample reasons to consider Ulysses *to be an obscene book.*

—Assistant District Attorney Samuel Coleman, from the case to ban James Joyce's *Ulysses*, 1933

FIVE KILOS OF MANGOS

OF ALL THE PRISONERS I MET, he was the happiest. On my third day inside, he drew me into conversation and told me the absurd story of his case, which made me laugh—the first laugh I'd managed since I arrived.

He was broad and thick limbed, with pale skin and a gleaming bald pate. He was charged with accepting a bribe, which he denied with absolute confidence. This man, a low-ranking employee at the Ministry of Agriculture, occupied the very bottom rung of the middle class; he had a son and two daughters, the eldest of whom was engaged to be married, hopefully very soon. The groom's family had no idea he was in prison, even though he'd been absent for quite a long time, and his relatives simply continued to say he was working on a contract in the Gulf. Such was his faith that he'd be found not guilty that he instructed his family to fix the date of the wedding for two weeks after his hearing.

"So you really didn't take the money?" I asked him jokingly.

He guffawed loudly as he stuffed a piece of bread heaped with beans into his mouth.

"Well, if I did, where the heck is it?" he spluttered. "Why can't they tell us that? And anyway, if I had that kind of money, would I be looking like this?"

"Hang on. You're accused of taking a bribe of five thousand pounds," I said, laughing. This sum equaled only about two hundred and sixty bucks. "Let's say you did take it. Would it make that much of a difference to how you're looking?"

The single piece of evidence in his case was a recorded phone call between him and an associate of his department. The call had been uncovered during an internal investigation by the Administrative Control Authority, whose job it was to internally police other governmental departments. Before saying goodbye and hanging up, the associate, who was calling from the city of Isma'iliyya, politely asked if he needed anything from there.

"How about five kilos of mangos?" joked the man spontaneously, since Isma'iliyya was famed for its mango orchards.

For these prospective five kilos of mangos, which the authorities became convinced were a code, the man had spent twenty-two months in prison waiting for his hearing. Despite this, he was upbeat, blithely confident that he'd be found not guilty, which I found pretty surprising. Some of the other prisoners, in particular those who'd worked in other ministerial departments like his, asked me to try to prepare him for a different outcome, seeing as he and I were quite close. When the Administrative Control Authority decided to frame someone, it only ever went one way, they said, and that way was a guilty verdict; what was more, the youngest son of the president had worked on the prosecuting team, and no judge was going to rule not guilty against the wishes of the son of 'Abd al-Fattah al-Sisi himself. After all, it was in the power of the ACA to monitor the judges themselves, and probably also to arrest them if they felt like it.

We heard the news from the intelligence officers while he was still at the prison gate: seven years. I lay down on my top bunk, swallowed a Panadol Night, and closed my eyes to try to sleep. I didn't want to see him. This hideous reality was more than I could bear. I was too exhausted from resisting the rot, from constantly trying to scrape and scrub it from my body.

It was the only time I ever considered suicide while in prison. Suicide, I thought, would free me from all the rage and hatred I felt toward this country.

EGYPT THE OLD SOW

A tide began to surge beneath the calm surface of Stephen's friendliness.

—This race and this country and this life produced me, he said. I shall express myself as I am.

—Try to be one of us, repeated Davin. In heart you are an Irishman but your pride is too powerful.

—My ancestors threw off their language and took another, Stephen said. They allowed a handful of foreigners to subject them. Do you fancy I am going to pay in my own life and person debts they made? What for?

—For our freedom, said Davin.

—No honourable and sincere man, said Stephen, has given up to you his life and his youth and his affections from the days of Tone to those of Parnell, but you sold him to the enemy or failed him in need or reviled him and left him for another. And you invite me to be one of you. I'd see you damned first.

—They died for their ideals, Stevie, said Davin. Our day will come yet, believe me.

Stephen, following his own thought, was silent for an instant.

—The soul is born, he said vaguely, first in those moments I told you of. It has a slow and dark birth, more mysterious than the birth of the body. When the soul of a man is born in this country there are nets flung at it to hold it back from flight. You talk to me of nationality, language, religion. I shall try to fly by those nets.

Davin knocked the ashes from his pipe.

—Too deep for me, Stevie, he said. But a man's country comes first. Ireland first, Stevie. You can be a poet or a mystic after.

—Do you know what Ireland is? asked Stephen with cold violence. Ireland is the old sow that eats her farrow.

—James Joyce, *A Portrait of the Artist as a Young Man*

Day 237: Friday, October 14, 2016

I've just been sent a copy of Mona Kareem's poetry collection *What I Sleep for Today*. She writes: "I want to put my loved ones in my pocket so I can kiss them every minute."

Day 260: Sunday, November 6, 2016

I've made decent progress on the novel. Writing with pen and paper is harder work than I'd remembered, or maybe it's just the snaillike positions I'm forced to sit in, thigh as desk, when writing. Something releases itself from my muscles and pours itself out onto the paper.

Day 272: Friday, November 18, 2016

Bad week. Didn't get anything done. Couldn't manage even
the basic workout I've been doing most days so far. I've barely
done any work on the novel this month either. And my stomach
isn't working properly. All thanks to the constant rumors of a
presidential pardon.

In the newspapers we get delivered, on TV, and here in
prison itself, there's talk of little else but the supposed plans
to issue a presidential pardon for prisoners in freedom-of-ex-
pression cases. Some of the prisoners, and even the odd guard,
have actually been congratulating me to my face when they see
me. At visiting time, one officer said the matter was as good as
decided: "You'll be home in a few days," he assured me. All this
hope is too much for my nerves, and no matter how much I try
to keep it out of my mind, it just keeps coming back. But what
makes me most anxious isn't the torment of hoping itself; it's
the thought of what that torment is doing to my mom and to
Yasmine. Yasmine especially: I am terrified at what this long,
terrible wait is doing to her health.

BANGING MY HEAD
AGAINST THE MIRROR

LIKE ANYBODY WHO GIVES A shit about the public good in Egypt, I expected to go to prison at some point. There's always the possibility you'll be grabbed off the street at a demonstration—or even not at a demonstration—or be detained for some opinion you've expressed or stance you've taken. It was just a tax I tried to evade.

I ended up going to prison anyway—but for writing literature, not journalism. I was still hesitant to call myself a writer right up till the point I went to prison. I always felt that what I wrote wasn't good enough, didn't satisfy my own ambitions; I still do. I was embarrassed to talk about literature and my own work. As far as I was concerned, the tiny circle of friends I wrote for was my audience, and without their enthusiasm and insistence, I never would have published or carried on down this path.

My high school graduation results were poor—a nasty shock for my family, who'd planned to offer up their firstborn at the altar of medical school. My nickname since childhood had been "Doctor": not just because my father, uncle, and cousins were all either doctors or studying to be, but also because my father, a pediatrician, was an especially beloved figure in our hometown, and it was a given that I'd take over his clinic. When my grades came in, it must have looked like I'd failed on purpose. There weren't any universities I wanted to go to or any subjects I felt like studying—the only thing I knew was that there was no way in hell I was going to medical school.

In the preferences booklet we had to fill out and hand to the ranking and admissions office, I spotted a notice for the Daily News Academy, a training college run by one of the country's biggest newspapers, which offered a degree in journalism. With the support and encouragement of 'Abd al-Nasir Sayyid, my high school Arabic teacher, who became a good friend, that's what I chose to do, while he shouldered the task of persuading my dad.

I picked journalism because it seemed to be the closest thing to what I wanted to do, and that—what a fool!—was writing. I wrote poetry at the time, and later, at university, my friend Ahmed Wael and I became obsessed with open and hybrid texts. We used to spend whole nights and days in hallucinatory literary trances, taking turns working on a single shared text while we smoked and listened to music. The literature we craved was untamable and uncontainable. It celebrated error rather than fetishizing correctness, let you wander and get lost instead of dispensing wisdom.

When I discovered blogging, I found a way to do all that. Publishing anonymously, I lived a double life for many years after graduating. I had a day job at *Literature Review* as a junior reporter covering arts and culture, writing in a stuffy, formal, and information-packed style that was decidedly unambitious in its message. One day, as we rode the elevator up to the news-paper offices, my colleague Mansoura Ez Eldin, who is also a novelist, asked me innocently, "Do you have a blog called *Shadow Puppet?*"

I had no idea how she'd guessed it was me, or how she'd even found the blog, but she told me she liked it and complimented my writing. "I don't see why you don't just write like that," she added. A few months later I gave her the manuscript of *Rogers*, a long text I was thinking of publishing on my blog, accompanied by Pink Floyd songs. It was she who said, "This is a great novel." Encouraged by her support, I uploaded it as a free pdf file on my blog.

To my surprise, I received an offer to publish the novel a few days later from Muhammad Sharqawi, the founder of a press called Malamih. But even after it was published, I still didn't engage seriously with the literary world, other than when I was covering it as a journalist.

Writing, for me, has always been a thing of whim, captive to my mood swings and urges. I write under the intense pressure of an internal impulse; I don't write regularly or with the aim of creating grand structures. I write to reach out to the people I'm closest to. I'm always amazed when I meet someone I don't know and they tell me they've read and enjoyed something of mine, because I just can't imagine how it could interest anyone other than my friends.

Prison put an end to all these immature ideas. Like every prisoner with a modicum of education and self-regard, I became absorbed in searching for myself. I stood in front of the cell-block's only mirror, which hung on a nail over the sink, and peered into my own eyes, looking for the Ahmed I wanted, or the Ahmed that wanted me.

The thing is, in prison, you don't find yourself or come to understand yourself. Instead, you beat yourself up for every decision that brought you to where you are today. You get mad and scream at yourself and bash your head against the mirror. Was it really worth it? Is the written word worth so huge a sacrifice? The daily abuse and humiliation, the cockroaches that scuttle over your body while you sleep? And if you decide it's worth it for you, what about your family and the people who love you? Do they deserve to be put through this miserable, exhausting ordeal? There were many times I wasn't sure if being a writer was really my vocation, or if prison had forced my hand.

That said, during the controversy over my book, I was bitterly disappointed by the pathetic stance of the Journalists' Union and the Journalism Association. With the exception of Khalid al-Balshi and Muhammad Kamil from the union's board, their support was lukewarm and furtive. By total contrast, the

Writers' Union—of which I wasn't even a member—offered their unconditional solidarity, as did the wider literary community.

Prison was also a wake-up call to the fact that I was past thirty and still hadn't made up my mind what I wanted to do. Enough fucking about, Ahmed, I thought one evening as I stared at the flaking ceiling of my cell. The literary world is up in arms, and you're in the middle of it. You're a writer now. You have to start taking it seriously.

PROUST FINDS
HIS LOST TIME

EXCEPT, OF COURSE, EVERYONE GETS a taste for writing in prison. In my early days on the cellblock, I noticed one elderly inmate who slept with a pile of notebooks stacked next to him. I would regularly pass by his bunk and find him withdrawn, hunched over his writing in deep concentration. I had no idea what he was writing, but his commitment to the craft felt like a challenge. When I saw him writing I'd go back to my bunk and stare at a blank sheet of paper for an hour, thinking about the novel I wanted to write, then scribble one line before lying down to light a cigarette and gaze at the shapes the smoke made in the air above me.

One day, I summoned the nerve to engage my notebook-collecting cellmate in conversation.

"Excuse me. Would it be okay if I asked you a question?" I ventured.

"Of course, Mr. Naji!" he replied. "Goodness me. Shall I make you a cup of tea?"

"Thanks, no need. I just wondered: What is it you write about all day?"

A broad smile spread across his face as he told me he was writing his memoirs. A lot of people assumed he was spying on his cellmates and reporting everything they said to the administration, he explained, but really he was just keeping a journal. He opened a notebook and held it out for me to read a page. It was a meticulously kept account of his daily life, each section beginning with a date, followed by the time he woke up, and then every single thing he'd done that day.

"Went to bathroom. Fried egg and milky tea for breakfast today. Spent some time reading Shaykh Sha'rawi's *The Prayer That Is Answered.*" Here he had copied down the paragraphs he'd read, and then it went on: "Talked to ―― about his job as an airport engineer, saw in newspaper that there are protests in Venezuela—country on verge of bankruptcy. Played ping-pong in rec hour. Beat ――." The man had six notebooks of this stuff, all written in a small, neat hand. He had diligently recorded everything he'd seen, read, and eaten, and even the times and details of his bowel movements, e.g.: "Water off today so borrowed ――'s bucket to go to bathroom. Passed water and evacuated."

Keeping a firm grip on myself, I closed the notebook. Life's a weird one. I asked him if he'd ever heard of a writer called Marcel Proust. He hadn't, of course, but mentioned another

French writer he knew of, Sartre. That was someone else, I told him. "The point is, Proust used to write like you."

Although he recorded everything, he confided, not everything he wrote was fit to publish. He recorded so as to remember, because he didn't want to forget a single day of his life in prison and because he'd seen so much injustice, so many repeated and accumulated injustices, in fact, that he felt it was his duty to reveal them, and he was waiting to get out of prison so he could begin the task of reviewing his notebook memoirs with a view to choosing which parts should be published.

Sometime later, Marcel received notice of his imminent release. He packed up his belongings, shook everyone's hands, bequeathed me one of his pens, and left the cellblock. At the prison gate, where he was searched before leaving, the chief of intelligence found the notebooks.

"What are these?"

"My memoirs," replied Proust.

"No way," said the chief of intelligence. "That's against the rules. I can't let these leave the premises."

Proust was dumbfounded, and the chief of intelligence almost as much so. He couldn't confiscate the notebooks, or Proust would accuse him of theft, but he could hardly allow them—and the detailed documentation they contained of everything that went on in his prison—to leave the facility. He decided that Proust would have to get rid of the memoirs; otherwise, he himself wouldn't be allowed to leave.

With hot tears streaming down his face, Proust stood in the prison yard, tore apart his notebooks, and cast the bundled pages into a roaring fire that had been lit inside a battered oil drum. "God will be my sufficiency and the best of all providers," he repeated fervently as the pages burned.

By that point I'd written the first chapter of my new novel, and when I heard what had happened to Proust, I was stricken with panic. I had to keep it a secret that I was writing, I had to hide the manuscript carefully, and I had to make sure I'd manage to smuggle it out, or else I'd lose everything, like Marcel. They would steal my memories, force me to wipe everything I remembered of prison, and turn my torment into a void that I couldn't even go back and look at.

Day 95: Wednesday, May 25, 2016

In the early nineteenth century, during the reign of Mehmet Ali Pasha, prisoners used to be tattooed on their shoulder with the letter *L* for *Liman Tura*—Tura Prison. Runaway naval conscripts were tattooed with a ship and anchor if they were caught. Even today, when prison intelligence receives a new prisoner charged with a felony, they ask him if he has any "marks," and strip him to check if he has any tattoos from other prisons.

FOLDING BONES

THREE WEEKS IN, I FOUND A buddy.

It's hard to get by alone in prison. For example, we never had enough fruit and vegetables, and in an environment as unhealthy as that, you need your vitamins. I got a visit from my family every two weeks, when they'd bring fruit and vegetables, among other things, but in the heat and humidity they went bad within days, and I couldn't keep them in the refrigerator, because the refrigerator was reserved for meat. By buddying up with someone else, or a group of people, you could share your food deliveries and that way guarantee that everyone in the group would have fresh food throughout the week.

My buddy, HB, occupied the bunk next to mine. The bunks in the cellblock were made of reinforced concrete and separated from one another by a concrete block about ten centimeters high. On the divider between our bunks we kept a cardboard box where we stored packets of sugar, coffee, tea, Nescafé, and sometimes cookies. Next to this box were my books. I kept my papers and writing notebooks under the mattress.

By the light of the same jerry-rigged bulb under which I read the Arabic translation of Salman Rushdie's *Midnight's Children*, my buddy stayed up late writing long, multipage letters in blue ink on a legal pad, now and then taking out a corrector pen, which he rattled before erasing a mistake or a line he'd thought better of. His letter-writing habit was obsessive, and I envied his physical ability to write for hours on end. I've always struggled to hold a pen and write for long periods, and in school exams I often wrote short summary answers instead of putting down everything I knew, just because my hand got tired. As a teenager I started writing short stories and journals on the computer, and after graduating from university, I abandoned pen and paper completely. In prison, I had to learn all over again how to grip a pen and write by hand on lined paper.

This was how our setup worked. First, my buddy and I managed to buy an old copy of *Gulf Flower*, an upscale, well-produced Emirati society magazine that was perfect for leaning on as we wrote. We used to keep it on the concrete divider between our bunks, and he also stored the many pages of his letters inside it; being shorter than me, he could write leaning on the divider, but when I tried, every bone and muscle in my back hurt within minutes. By experimenting, I found it easiest to sit with my back to the wall, my knees bent, and *Gulf Flower* resting on my thighs. This was how I wrote.

I divided my writing sessions so as not to tire myself out too quickly. After one paragraph, I'd stretch and shake out my body so it wouldn't suddenly seize up on me. My knees began to click, and in the night I was sometimes awoken by the pain, caused by the cold and damp and the uncomfortable bed. Whenever I tried to stretch out, my legs hit the end of the bunk because I was too tall. I would stay awake talking to the aches in my body, hoping they would go away so I could fall back asleep. In the morning, every movement would hurt, and I'd grit my teeth against the pain in my bent knees as I sat down again with my ballpoint pen and my notebook resting on my thighs.

Every word I wrote in that awkward, tiring position carries the ache and the effort it cost me. This is what it is to be a writer, I thought. Practice it. This is your life—be prepared to use it.

CHEWING TIME

REACH OUT AND GRAB A piece of time. Tear off the biggest piece you can manage, then fold it in half. Fold that in half again so you have a quarter, and keep folding until you can't fold it any smaller, then put it into your mouth. Chew it slowly, try to get the juice out of it, turn it over with your tongue so it moves around in your mouth. You keep chewing but nothing happens. Time doesn't melt or disintegrate. You close your eyes and open them again and the fingers on the clock haven't even moved. You force yourself to look away and start inventing things to do to pass the time. Anything.

On one inspection, they confiscated our chess sets. The devoted chess players looked at one another, sighing in exasperation and slapping one hand against another like that would make the boredom go away. Finally one of them had an idea. He took the standard-issue soap we were given and began carving it into individual pieces, and in two days we had a full set; then, with some felt-tip pens his family had brought, he colored the two sets of pieces blue and yellow. Another of our cellmates talked to one of the felons who worked in the prison factory and managed to get hold of a white ceramic tile. He carefully drew squares on it using a ruler and a black marker. In the end we had a chessboard and pieces that we'd fashioned entirely by ourselves, and we were extremely proud.

We played against time on many occasions, but it always won, because no matter how long the game lasted or how engrossing it was, it always came to an end, and even if it didn't, you always knew that sooner or later the nabatshi would turn out the lights and play would have to stop.

Day 56: Saturday, April 16, 2016

Devoured four really good books in two days: *Roses and Ash*, the letters of Mohamed Choukri and Mohamed Berrada; Charles Bukowski's *South of No North*, translated into Arabic by Amani Lazare; *The Way of Loneliness* by Tuna Kiremitçi, translated by Khalid Mikkawi; and *A House Full of Crazy People*, an anthology of *Paris Review* interviews with Milan Kundera, Susan Sontag, Naguib Mahfouz, Henry Miller, Jorge Luis Borges, Ernest Hemingway, and others, translated by Ahmad Shafi'i.

Day 59: Tuesday, April 19, 2016

I've run out of books and had to go back to the prison library.

Read two novellas by Yusuf Idris, *New York 80* and *Vienna 60*. So irritating and pathetic! A film from the "clean cinema" school of the early 2000s is livelier and more authentic than either of these.

Day 61: Thursday, April 21, 2016

Boredom and frustration are sticking in my throat and leaving a bitter taste on my tongue. Missing Yasmine is unlike anything I've felt before. Dreams are the only means of escape I have, and it's getting harder to have them. The administration's harassment is sapping all the patience and resolve I have left. It's so suffocating that I'm scared to write about it here, in case my notebook falls into the wrong hands or gets confiscated and I land myself in trouble.

Day 65: Monday, April 25, 2016

There's no place for lazy people or daydreamers. They're thought of as failures. And if they try to encourage the same subversive desires in others, the state will come down on them with the full force of its violence—a violence codified and sanctified by law, needless to say.

As far as progress goes, the tools of coercion and control have become more refined, which is to say less and less visible to the populace. The primary function of these tools is to guarantee the maintenance of private property and increase the productivity of modern industrialized society.

Day 68: Thursday, April 28, 2016

Out of the blue, A asked me over dinner why we were here.
I thought he meant why we were here in prison. Turned out he
meant in *existence*.

FALTERING

BEFORE I WENT TO PRISON I WAS thinking of writing a historical novel. After *Using Life* came out, I had gotten interested in the nineteenth century, the era when all the great ideas were born and died. The novel I had in mind was going to be called *Faltering*. Once I was allowed to receive books, I asked my friend Ahmed Wael to bring me everything he could find on the nineteenth century, and especially the history of Saint-Simonianism, a French political, religious, and social movement that influenced the creation of the Suez Canal.

Emboldened by my decision to "be a writer," I started working on the book in prison—mainly so as to feel like I wasn't wasting my time, but also because reading and writing wove themselves into a sort of cocoon that deflected the gossip, trivial ideas, and pointless conversations that went on around me, and also seemed to keep out the heat, humidity, moldy smells, and the varied and peculiar insect life with which we shared our living quarters.

I earnestly set about reinventing, on paper, the human experience of history. Two pages in, I went over what I'd written and discovered that there were mistakes and lots of things I wanted to change—but I hadn't left any room for corrections. After that I made sure to use only every other line, so that the blank lines could be spaces for editing and revising. I wrote in three colors: blue for the first draft; black for corrections, additions, and deletions; and red for comments about the structure of the plot and connections between events.

By this laborious method, I finished the first chapter in a month. I encountered a new problem in chapter two, when I found I wanted to move a paragraph from chapter one. So I came up with a cataloging system that involved numbering every page in the notebook, and then each paragraph on each page. That made it easier to shift sections around. If I wanted, for example, to move paragraph 3 on page 12 to just before paragraph 5 on page 28, I'd put a note before paragraph 5, on page 28, saying "3 p. 12." One day, I knew, I'd get out of prison, and when that day came, I would sit with my laptop at a table and chair fit for human use, instead of at a makeshift desk of leg bones, to transcribe and rewrite the whole novel from prison notebook to computer screen.

The novel evolved, and soon it was no longer about the nineteenth century in particular but about Kamil Ru'ba Laz, the main character in Naguib Mahfouz's novel *The Mirage*, which

I'd just read for the first time in prison. The book is a psychological study of a man strangely attached to his mother, and Kamil's character turned out to be modeled on a real person, who was furious at the liberties Mahfouz had taken with his identity. In my own book, I imagined Kamil entering a world of sensual pleasures with a woman called 'Atiyyat, after the death of his mother and betrayal of his wife. In response to Naguib Mahfouz's character assassination, Kamil decides to write his own life story, but is arrested and imprisoned for offenses against public morals. In prison, he again begins to write, and the novel alternates between his prison diaries and the unfolding story of a group of followers of the Church of Modernity, Science, and Labor, who make their way to Egypt in search of a "mystical union between the body of the West and the spirit of the East." They plan to construct a city of the future, between the Red Sea and the Mediterranean, which will control international trade, reshape the global economy, and direct the course of human life for the better.

With the switch from computer to pen and paper, I discovered new horizons of style and syntax. Deliberately keeping my sentences short—since I knew what I was writing was only a rough copy—I was unencumbered by lyricism and finished a full first draft of the novel. Sometimes I even abbreviated whole paragraphs. When I read my work back to myself, it felt like a new form, a new voice; I was surprised and pleased with the unexpected layers of richness that were now within my reach.

When I got out of prison and sat down to rewrite it all, I felt my sentences stretching out, becoming convoluted, dragging their feet. I lost my grip on the story; the plotlines disintegrated and stopped making sense. Sitting at my laptop, I'd puzzle over the words I was rewriting, my memory faltering: was the sentence so short because I'd intended it to be? Or because my arm muscles had started to hurt, the ache in my knees was getting to be too much, and I'd just wanted to take a break from writing? When is it the mind that thinks and writes, and when is it the body?

YOU HAVE TO PUSH IF YOU WANT TO GIVE BIRTH TO LITERATURE

I STRIPPED AND SQUATTED AS if to piss, keeping well away from the stinking hole of the squat toilet. Closing my eyes to concentrate, I held my breath, tensed my muscles, and pushed. I could feel the pressure on my insides, but with no result. Nothing came out. I took another breath and repeated, first gently and then gradually with more force. I could feel it in my rectum this time, but still nothing came out.

As I pushed harder, the end of the plastic bag appeared from out of my anus. It hurt, but with each push, more of the bag emerged and the sense of relief grew stronger. When enough of it had appeared, I tugged on the end of the bag with two fingers, pushing at the same time, and with the help of the hair cream I'd applied beforehand, the entire package slid out. It was an easy delivery, and the thin cylinder of folded paper in its plastic wrapping was only lightly flecked with shit.

I turned on the shower and rinsed off the shit and left-over hair cream as best I could under the thin stream of water. I gently smoothed out the plastic bag and watched as the tight wad of paper inside unfurled.

Day 14: Saturday, March 5, 2016

Since I arrived, A has always moaned in his sleep. He's sick and consumes only liquids. He goes to see the prison doctor every day for an injection. I tried to find out what's wrong with him at one point; apparently, it's some complicated stomach condition that requires surgery, and the prison administration won't let him out to have it done. He's missing his left eye. During one of the rare hours when he wasn't fainting with pain, I asked him whether he'd lost his eye in prison. "No," he replied. "This one went in the revolution."

He was unemployed when the revolution of January 25, 2011, came about, and although he wasn't interested in politics at first, he became more and more involved in political events as time went on. After the revolution, he *got* politics. One day, the house phone rang and he was summoned to appear at a government office. When he arrived, he found himself in a large hall with others who had been injured during the revolution. A functionary appeared and started speechifying, promising to give them jobs and send them on umrah. He decided he'd let his father take the umrah trip instead, but in the end neither he nor his father went anywhere, because that part of the promise turned out to be a pack of lies.

Months went by before another telephone call informed him he'd been appointed to a low-ranking administrative position—the very lowest rank possible—in a state office somewhere, which he accepted. He didn't get any training and nobody told him what he was meant to be doing, so he just copied his colleagues and followed orders, but after less than eight months on the job, he was arrested and charged with accepting bribery.

So far he's been in detention for eighteen months. He's awaiting trial for allegedly receiving a bribe of one hundred and fifty Egyptian pounds—just under ten dollars. Usually, cases involving bribes of anything under a thousand pounds are dismissed by the public prosecutor, but A was sent to May 15 Prison for six months.

Universally feared, May 15 Prison is a slaughterhouse. No home cooking is allowed to be brought in on visits, so all you get is prison food. In the mornings they throw a ladleful of cooked beans onto a grubby sheet of newspaper, a heap of bread on top of that, and that's breakfast; in the afternoons they dump rice on the floor, vegetables on top, and that's lunch. There's no cutlery, not even plastic; you eat with your hands, like an animal, and you urinate in a hole, like an animal. Inmates live thirty or forty to a tiny cell, and the space you're given for sleeping is just over a handspan wide.

There are degrees of hell: let's not forget that there are distinctions between us.

SLEEPING BESIDE
THE PINK DRAGON

ON NEW YEAR'S EVE 2006, I was invited to a party at the house
of two friends, Ahmad and Amr Gharbeia. We stayed up till
the early hours, dancing and drinking and designing blogs and
downloading Ubuntu and other open-source software. At the end
of the night, we all fell asleep scattered around the house, and
I ended up on the floor beneath a statue of our friends' father, who
was a sculptor. Next to me was Alaa Abd el-Fattah.

The party attendees were a mix of bloggers, writers, pro-
grammers, university students, and doctors, from a range of
different social backgrounds. We'd been brought together
by our rage at the political and social situation, our belief in
human rights and freedom of expression, and our devotion
to the internet and open-source software. Among the group,
the people I was closest to at the time were Alaa and his then
wife, Manal.

Most of us lived double lives. I was in the last year of my studies and working as a trainee journalist at *Literature Review*. By day, I edited news pieces that praised President Mubarak and his policies and feted the cultural and educational projects of the First Lady. By night, I'd hang out with Alaa, plotting how we could design a spoof of the official presidential website that would be full of satirical content.

I blogged under the name Iblis—Satan. We all had pen names and hid our real identities, apart from Alaa, who not only wrote under his real name but often mentioned details of his life and even posted pictures of himself and his family. He was possessed with a courage and directness that affronted some people, who took it as egotistical or rude, and he had an innate skill for leadership and management, which, combined with his intelligence, meant he could lead you without you even noticing you were being led. As far as I am concerned, Alaa's only failing is that he's never wanted to be a leader; he has always preferred to be a free individual who can inspire others, and even though he's been offered leadership positions on more than one occasion, he's always turned his back on them.

But it wasn't because of politics that I became close with Alaa; it was because of music. He was the only person in Egypt who had all the albums of Soapkills, Yasmine Hamdan and Zeid Hamdan's legendary band. Since he and Manal lived just five minutes from me, I often went over there to have dinner or beers and watch films or borrow books. It was Alaa who first got me hooked on graphic novels, introducing me to Alan Moore,

Neil Gaiman, Ahmed Ibrahim Hegazy, Bahgat Othman, and many other writers, both local and international, and as a result, I started attempting to write graphic novels myself and ended up including illustrations in *Using Life*.

At that New Year's party, Alaa and I kept putting Arabic music on, to the annoyance of our friends, who mostly wanted to listen to rock and jazz. While we were dancing to a song by Ahmed 'Adawiyya, our friend Nora Younis came in and breathlessly told us that the police had massacred the Sudanese refugees camping out at the UN Refugee Agency's Cairo headquarters. In the months prior, more than two thousand Sudanese refugees had gathered there, and that night the Egyptian security forces opened fire on the crowd, killing more than twenty-five, and wounding one hundred and sixty-nine. In the aftermath of the massacre, the blogosphere challenged the dishonest government narrative parroted by the mainstream media, and came to function as an alternative media source for the first time. Bloggers also began to write about sectarian conflict and the repression and racism faced by Egypt's Christians, about sexual violence against women, and about the silenced voices of queer people. They criticized Mubarak by name and mocked his regime and its policies. Alaa and his partner had designed a blog, known first as *Manal and Alaa's Bit Bucket* and later as the *Egyptian Blog Aggregator*, which hosted a feed of everything published on the Egyptian blogosphere. This earned Alaa his designation as "the spiritual father of Egyptian blogs," along with the nickname "the Pink Dragon."

In May 2006, Alaa took part in a series of demonstrations supporting the judiciary, who were demanding greater autonomy from the executive branch. I didn't share his position; in my view, the judiciary were part and parcel of the regime, a site of autocratic power in and of themselves, and nothing would induce me to take their side. I was visiting my family in al-Mansura when I saw the news on the *Egyptian Blog Aggregator*: the police had arrested dozens of demonstrators, among them Alaa.

I felt an ice-cold stab to my heart. It was the first time prison had seized someone who was dear to me. It took me several hours to pull myself together and call Manal to confirm the news; I can still remember how I stammered as I fumbled for the right words. Arabic has so many stock phrases—for illness, death, childbirth, weddings, birthdays, the new year—but what do you say when someone's been swallowed up by prison?

Alaa spent forty-five days there, and by the time he came out, his fame had spread beyond the blogosphere and into the political arena. That he was young and spoke excellent English made him appealing to US and European media outlets, which interviewed him widely. But he didn't want to be a politician: he was a programmer and activist, and had no interest in playing the political game. Career prospects in the very primitive Egyptian tech sector were limited, too, and soon Alaa found a good job in South Africa, where he and Manal lived for years, until they returned to Egypt in the wake of the 2011 revolution.

In the heady atmosphere that followed the uprising, our paths diverged. I found myself in disagreement with Alaa over some of the groups and policies he supported—like the constitutional referendum that took place in March 2011—and we fell out of touch, though our mutual respect and affection remained.

Alaa was a vocal critic of the military and its involvement in politics. Several times, they tried to silence him, but he became the face and leader of the revolution. In 2014, after the military coup, when Field Marshal Sisi became president, Alaa was arrested and sentenced to five years in prison. The official accusation was that he'd broken a demonstration law by participating in a protest held without permission. He wasn't even at the protest in question, but that wasn't a problem for the authorities.

When I went to prison, one of the first things my cellmates told me was that Alaa was in the cellblock next door, and I soon received my welcome gift from him via the fixer. The next day at recreation, I walked toward the locked cellblock gate to say hello, but the second I stopped, I found guards coming at me from every direction. "Get back!" they yelled. "What are you doing? You're under strict orders not to speak to Alaa!"

This state of affairs continued for five months: we weren't allowed to speak or be in any contact at all, but when we occasionally passed each other in the visiting room, we'd smile and sometimes manage to exchange a few words before the guards came along and separated us.

One morning after my first five months, we were woken up and told to gather our belongings and move to a different cellblock. I picked up my mattress and we marched through to cellblock 2/1, where Alaa was held. I was already taken aback at being put in the same cell as Alaa; then the cellblock nabatshi—who also happened to be the prison's chief nabatshi—told me I was to take the bunk above his. Alaa and I had to laugh: we simply couldn't fathom the machinations of power that had brought this about. Why would they keep us apart so vigilantly for months, then decide to put me right next to him?

A decade after that New Year's party, I was sleeping next to the Pink Dragon again.

A CURTAIN OF
ONE'S OWN

WHEN ALAA AND I BECAME BUNK neighbors, we resumed
our old conversations and arguments immediately, raising our
voices in disagreement over the future of the internet, or the
question of whether companies like Uber were going to save
the world or take it prisoner. Our cellmates didn't really get
what these discussions were about; sometimes one of the birds
would shuffle over and inquire, "How come you and Alaa were
shouting at each other yesterday?" I didn't know how to explain
that we'd been debating the prospects of open-source software
and whether or not the battle against big tech was already lost.

Alaa had developed a disciplined routine for prison life. He
spent most of his time with headphones on, pacing the narrow
passage inside the cellblock to keep his muscles moving. He'd
been there for two and a half years and he had even longer
to go. He shared the wisdom he'd accumulated about how to

AHMED NAJI

survive and maintain your sanity within the four walls of the cell; his company was like a balm on hard days, and it lessened the burden of time's sluggish progress.

A month and a half after I was moved to Alaa's cell, they moved me again: to the lower bunk right next to his. I was delighted. Alaa remarked something to the effect of "Humans are animals. They can adapt to anything." He was right: I had adapted so well to being in prison that this marginal improvement in my circumstances felt like a huge win.

I hung a line the length of the bunk and folded an old bedsheet over it. Inside, with the bedsheet as a curtain, I was finally by myself. It was the first privacy I'd had since I'd arrived in prison. I stripped down and slept butt naked behind my curtain. I spent most of the daytime hours reading, writing in my diary, writing letters, or working on my new novel. Sometimes I borrowed Alaa's radio and headphones, and that meant I could listen to music. Alaa had a precious personal library, too, including books in English, a collection of comics and graphic novels in both Arabic and English, and a large Oxford dictionary, which I used to brush up on my English and memorize new vocabulary.

CENSORSHIP

THE CHIEF OF INTELLIGENCE HAD the final say on which books we could and couldn't borrow. Any magazine or newspaper that mentioned my name or covered my case wasn't allowed in, and the same went for any book that bore my name. While in prison, I clung stubbornly to the goal of publishing my short story collection, "The Case of the Missing Liver." I wanted to fool myself into believing that my ideas had wings, and a butthole to poop from as they flew. But, of course, the chief of intelligence wouldn't let any of the drafts I'd prepared earlier enter the prison.

I ended up asking two writer friends, Ahmed Wael and Nael Eltoukhy, to do me the favor of editing the book. I asked them to come back to me on any points of disagreement, and so Yasmine frequently showed up for visits with notes asking me what I meant by a certain word, or informing me that Wael had found a mistake and suggested rephrasing the sentence to such and such, and either I'd agree or we'd spend some time discussing the options.

But things got more absurd. The chief of intelligence objected to Chuck Palahniuk's novel *Survivor* on the grounds that its Arabic title, *Al-Naji al-Akhir*, contained my name. After my family visited, if the officer was in a good mood, he would occasionally allow me to go into his office and choose from among the books they'd brought. He would entertain himself and his assistant by making fun of me and the books, and naturally I had to smile and laugh at all his idiotic jokes. Once, his eye was drawn to a book of the letters of Hannah Arendt and her sometime lover Martin Heidegger, the cover of which showed an image of a concentration camp surrounded by barbed-wire fences, in reference to Heidegger's dalliance with Nazism. His instinct for sniffing out security issues was instantly stirred.

"Is this about spies and that sort of thing?" he asked suspiciously.

I hesitated for a second, not sure what the right answer was. If I said yes, he might tell me that books about spies were banned; then again, calling it a spy novel might make it seem more innocuous than something that was actually about politics. I opted to play dumb.

"Spies? How do you mean?"

"You know, like espionage, action, escapes, all that stuff."

At this I realized he'd probably think the book might inspire some daredevil escape plan, so I hurried to correct him.

"No, no, it's actually a love story," I explained. "It's a collection of the love letters this couple wrote to each other."

"This whole thing is love letters?!" he scoffed, with all the wit and delicacy one would expect from an employee of the Egyptian security apparatus. "Couldn't they just meet up and get it on?"

I was at a loss to deal with the prison's censorship rules. So was Alaa. There were certain writers who were banned for everyone—Belal Fadl, for example, or Ibrahim Essa—but for "security-grade" prisoners like us, there was justification for prohibiting all sorts of books, and the decision lay in the hands of the chief of intelligence and his own personal appraisal of the risk involved. Eventually, Alaa and I decided to simply ask the fixer what the criteria were so that we didn't waste any more time requesting books that wouldn't be allowed in.

"I asked the boss," he replied simply. "He said Ahmed Naji isn't allowed anything smutty, and Alaa Abd el-Fattah isn't allowed anything about politics."

Alaa burst out laughing. "Well, that's easy, then. I'll order the X-rated stuff and Ahmed can get the politics!"

WHITE ROACHES

IN PRISON, I ENCOUNTERED SO MANY new kinds of insects: flies, mosquitoes, fleas, cockroaches, and, the most nightmarish of all, bedbugs. Seeing as there was no fresh air or sunlight in the cellblock, our beds quickly became infested, and so the ritual of airing out our mattresses in the sun at recreation time was held sacred. Sometimes we sprayed them with a mix of bleach and Dettol.

The prison regulations stated in no uncertain terms that a high standard of cleanliness and hygiene was to be maintained at all times, but of course that was the last thing the prison administration gave a crap about. I remember one time a young lawyer from the public prosecution, dressed in a smart black suit and white shirt, came on a routine inspection. When they opened the cellblock and he stepped inside, he clapped a tissue over his nose and mouth in pained disgust at the foul smells we were constantly forced to live with.

Once every two months during the summer, a contractor came to spray the bathrooms and kitchen with a powerful, vile-smelling chemical, and after that the insects would disappear for a few hours. That night, they'd reappear out of the open rubbish bins to take a stroll across the plates we ate from and over the underwear that was hung to dry on washing lines in the kitchen.

The most common pest was a small variety of cockroach, similar to the German cockroach, that got to only about a centimeter and a half long. The good news was that they didn't fly. The bad news was that they spread *fast*. Sometimes we had other kinds of cockroaches, like the large oriental type, which was at least two and a half centimeters long.

Before long, I got pretty used to the roaches, taking the old saying "Cockroaches are a prisoner's best friend" as my motto. One night I was reading *Paolo* by Youssef Rakha when suddenly I felt something on my shoulder in the dark, and looked down to find an enormous roach at least three centimeters long sitting there. I gave it a fraternal flick of the forefinger and it took off, zipping high into the air before settling again on the sleeping body of another cellmate. Sometimes you'd pick up the mattress you'd spent a while sitting or sleeping on and find a small family of cockroaches hanging out, making history underneath it. But the problem with cockroaches wasn't their general presence or the stench they gave off: it was the very real danger that one might crawl into your mouth while you were asleep and suffocate you to death.

The most dangerous of all was the white cockroach. According to the prison's health and safety regulations—at least, this was what I was told by one of the old-timers—if a white cockroach was ever found, it had to be immediately killed and its body preserved and handed over to the guard on duty, who would inform the authorities. Apparently, the presence of white roaches was an indicator of disease—scabies or worse—and that meant the prison's health officials would have to step in; otherwise, it would spread to the whole prison population. But of course that always happened anyway. Washing with sulfur soap seemed to be the only defense we had, and at one point I became obsessed: sulfur soap would be my salvation. This coincided with a period when rec hour was canceled because of some repairs going on in the building, and the result was that I got a whole load of other nasty skin conditions because I'd spent four months scrubbing myself with sulfur soap and not getting any sun.

Day 276: Tuesday, November 22, 2016

Just attended an extremely informative discussion between three colleagues—American, Kuwaiti, and Brazilian—on the cultivation and exportation of cocaine, the smuggling methods used, and the main lines of international distribution. The Kuwaiti, backed up by the American, told us that ships loaded with tons of cocaine idled alongside shipping routes in international waters, offering to sell to any buyer who could offload the goods and transport them. They also taught me an extremely important life lesson titled "Three ways to tell good coke from bad." Option one: Place a small quantity of coke on a piece of tinfoil, warm the tinfoil using a lighter, and watch for any changes of color in the coke. If it turns black, it's shit, but if it turns green or red, it's good stuff. Option two: Take a clear glass tumbler, fill it with ordinary cleaning bleach, and drop a tiny quantity of coke into it. If it sinks vertically, it's poor quality, but if it sinks in a spiral pattern, it's good. Our Brazilian cellmate objected to both these methods and offered a simple third option: rub the coke between your fingers until it produces oil, and take the quantity of oil as a marker of its quality.

USING THE RIGHT WORDS

SOMETIME IN THE EARLY TWENTIETH century, a large sub-group of Arabic words and expressions referring to sex and sexual organs began to disappear from printed books, as if the educated classes had signed a code of honor agreeing never to set them down on paper. This was why, when they found me guilty, the court of appeal would not record the turns of phrase I had used that they claimed to find so scandalizing. These words haven't vanished because speakers of Arabic have stopped using them, by the way; if anything, they're probably being used even more than before. It's only the immortality of being written down that is denied them.

Shunned by contemporary literature, the words gradually disappeared from new books. They were proscribed altogether from the lexicon of the newly coalescing Modern Standard Arabic that filled the airwaves and the pages of newspapers and magazines. They could be found in reprints and editions from the historical canon. But soon bowdlerized versions of those works, which omitted the offending words entirely, started turning up on the market. The words were chased not only out of literature but out of the entire realm of the written word, to be replaced by utilitarian terms like *penis* instead of *dick* or *cock*, and *vulva* in place of *cunt*. If the machine defined the modern period, then the genitalia, too, were to be reduced to mere functions.

To be clear, this repudiation wasn't because these words were too vernacular or low-class: I'm talking about words possessed of a fine classical pedigree, words that can be found in historical dictionaries and encyclopedias of the Arabic language. And at the same time, they're some of the most commonly used words for the sexual organs in a whole slew of contemporary Arabic dialects. Personally, I've never heard *anyone* use the Arabic equivalents of *penis* or *vagina*, and yet they're regularly bandied about in the written language. Part of the reason for this is colonization. After being subjected to decades of brutal rule by the Ottomans, the French, and the British, institutions of authority in Arab nations have attempted to erase indigenous terms and replace them with their European counterparts, declaring that the Arabic word for "cunt"—*kuss*—is obscene and pornographic, while *vagina* is perfectly acceptable.

Erotica and the various forms of writing that deal with sex never went away; they just had to make do without the correct, dictionary-sanctioned vocabulary that described the matters at hand in terms that people actually knew and used. Educated Arabs of the twentieth century created their own peculiar kind of language around sex, which used functional, instrumental terms, and was ornamented with rose garden metaphors that involved women revealing their "blossoms" and men savoring the juice of their "fruit." These were the kinds of descriptions of love that filled the Arabic novels of the period. But sex as pleasure, lust, motive, desire—once so common in Arabic literature—was confined to dusty books of the past.

While the West was masturbating furiously over the erotic tales of the *Nights* and the writings of Jalal al-Din al-Suyuti, Arabs themselves were burying those stories. What use did they have for tales of genies and flying carpets when they were attempting to liberate themselves from European occupation and colonization, armed with a national self-conception created in the image of European modernity and buttressed by essentially Victorian values?

These stories were forgotten and erased in favor of a more seemly version of the canon, and merely saying some of the words they used came to equal profanity and insult. These words have become freighted with all sorts of other negative implications, too, prime among them class connotations. Since the educated classes of the modern period have abandoned Arabic sex terms for English and French alternatives, these terms connote a speaker's proletarian vulgarity. No cultured, well-mannered person who's been brought up properly would ever use that sort of language!

Despite all this, written usage of these words exploded with increased access to the internet, first in the form of insults and expletives, and then in the erotica and pornographic writing that became so popular online. The genre was a crucible in which multiple dialects fused and readers encountered the rich variety of sexual language that each local version of Arabic had produced. The internet also saw morality campaigns that aimed to ban that same language, but they were no match for the frenzied outpouring of sexual self-expression by Arabic-speaking internet users who were damn well going to use their own words after being deprived of them for so long by respectable, educated elites.

These words are slowly returning to the world of literature too. They're peering out from behind the layers of shame imposed upon them by the Arab projects of enlightenment and modernity. For some commentators, this is tantamount to apostasy, and columns and think pieces fulminate on the moral backslide represented by internet obscenity, but what's happened is the opposite: people are liberating and reclaiming their language. Of course, it's hardly surprising that under the Sisi presidency, the establishment has reacted so cagily. Straining to regain control of the country after it nearly slipped from their grasp altogether, they're coming down harder than ever before on any sign of social or cultural rebellion.

The state avoids prosecuting solidly "political" cases, because those kinds of actions are readily perceived as state oppression, and run the risk of rallying the opposition. But the powers that be see social and cultural cases as a golden opportunity to flex their moral muscles and show society that they're defending family values. Like the public prosecution lawyer who was so obsessed with the sex scenes in my book, and the judge that found me guilty, they view these cases as a chance to paint themselves as defenders of morality, society, and the family—all of which are gravely threatened by writing. The powers that be think that when they blow the whistle of religion and morality, the masses will rush to fall in behind them. And they think that the unlucky victim who stands accused will simply keep their mouth shut, because how could such a filthy pervert dare to open their mouth once they've been shown for what they are?

The judge in my first trial was taken aback to find out we were going to call witnesses; they'd all been expecting us to be embarrassed and apologize. That's why their reaction was so hysterical when we went on the offensive and attacked them for overstepping their legal and constitutional role. In my second trial, the public prosecution lawyer screamed as he brandished a stack of my writings that had nothing to do with the case. Having tracked down everything I'd ever written online, he alleged that I had defended the use of the objectionable terms in question, and had even published an article in which I frankly announced that I was opposed to societal mores and values that constrained freedom of opinion and expression. He was so obsessed that at one point in his oral pleading, he turned to the bench and told them that on my website he'd found a short story called "La Señora," which he'd arbitrarily decided formed part of my novel *Using Life*, and then spent a tedious four minutes narrating the story. It centered on the same protagonist as the novel—when he said this, he pointed his finger at me—who has sex with a female drug dealer and helps her grow and sell hashish. I stared at the floor for the whole hearing, trying to hide behind my lawyers—Nasir Amin, Mahmoud Othman, and Yasmine—and hold in my laughter. The lawyer's performance reached its dramatic climax as he bellowed his demand that the harshest punishment possible be brought to bear upon me in order to avenge the families I'd destroyed, the children I'd corrupted, and the youths I'd cast into a pit of drug use and depravity. I had my hand clamped over my mouth, and I was so desperately stifling the urge to laugh that I ended up letting out a deafening fart instead.

Day 284: Wednesday, November 30, 2016

Extremely anxious. Trying to get over my fantasies of a presidential pardon. The date of our challenge at the court of cassation is approaching. I don't even know if I'm going to appear in court for the hearing or not. The guys here are saying no one gets sent to their appeal hearings. But if I don't, how will I know what the verdict is?

Day 290: Tuesday, December 6, 2016

The hearing's been postponed from December 4 to December 18 because the public prosecution hasn't submitted their brief. Apparently the judge called my lawyers "you human-rights lot." As far as I can understand, the cassation prosecution has accepted the paperwork for the appeal but hasn't submitted its opinion on the merits. The judge told them he wanted to hear oral statements and rule on the merits himself, so my lawyers requested a postponement that will give them time to see the public prosecutor's brief, once it's submitted, and prepare a detailed response.

I'm ignorant and confused, even more so than Kafka's man from the country, who spends his lifetime sitting before a gateway in the desert in the hope that it will open so he can seek the law.

Day 300: Friday, December 16, 2016

I dream a lot. I'm visited by friends and distant acquaintances, but Yasmine hasn't come to me in my dreams for a long time. I miss dreaming about her.

Day 303: Monday, December 19, 2016

Finally, by asking multiple sources, I've been able to find out that the court of cassation ruled that I should be released. It's confirmed—one of our cellmates even heard it on the radio—but the prison administration denies knowing anything.

"We've heard nothing," they say.

HUMILIATION

ONE MORNING WE WERE WOKEN up early and told to put on our uniforms and leave the cellblock. I opened my eyes. It was barely 6:00 a.m. All I could make out from the mutters of my cellmates was that there was a Prisons Authority inspection. Movement and muffled voices filtered in from outside, along with the unfamiliar sound of dogs barking.

I headed to the lavatory to wash my face and was standing in line for the sink when two plainclothes officers I'd never seen before burst in, yelling at us to get out, as they yanked open the curtains of each stall, kicked the trash cans over, and then dumped the pots and pans we used for cooking into the trash that now covered the ground.

I followed the others out, trying to avoid being seen by either of the demented officers. On my way to the door, I suddenly remembered the manuscript of my novel. Pretending to take a long slug from the plastic water bottle on my bed, I whipped the notebook out from under the mattress and quickly slid it into my bag of clothes. I don't know why that seemed a better hiding place. I guess I just thought a notebook in a bag would arouse less suspicion than a notebook under a mattress.

The Prisons Authority carried out surprise inspections every three months or so. The prison administration never knew when they would be. A squad from the Prisons Authority, reporting directly to the Ministry of the Interior, descended without warning and simply took over from the warden and his lieutenants. They reviewed the registers and paperwork, took all the keys, and went through every single cell. For the duration of the inspection, the prison was under the control of jailers we didn't know.

An officer in civilian clothes and a young lieutenant who held the inmate ID cards stood waiting as we filed out of our cells for the roll call. They checked that the card matched the prisoner by "half calling": the officer would shout the first part of your full name, and you had to reply with the second part.

"Ahmed Higazi!" yelled the officer.

"Saleh Naji!" I shouted back. But the lieutenant stopped me, glancing down at the card in his hand.

"What are you in for?"

"For writing, sir."

"What? Fighting?"

"No sir, writing. I'm a journalist and I wrote something."

"It says here 'gross violation of decency.' That means you raped or assaulted someone."

"No, sir. It was gross violation of public decency."

"Not a woman?"

"No, sir. Just the public."

I was shoved into a corner, and we were ordered to squat or sit on the ground. One man remained standing, and the young lieutenant bellowed at him to get down. He protested weakly that he had a problem with his knees, but before he could even finish the sentence the lieutenant whacked him in the face and he crumpled to the floor. They brought sniffer dogs, who inspected us thoroughly before being taken to the cellblock.

On the first floor, where they kept the felons, it was much more vicious. All we could hear was shouting and cursing, and the sound of mattresses and blankets being slashed apart with knives. One group of prisoners were made to strip and stand facing the wall.

We were kept there for about four hours. I spent the whole time willing myself to disappear. Violence like that had no reason or justification; it was a show of force, an unabashed delight in the pleasure of humiliating others. They really were dogs, rabid dogs, who tore up everything in their path as they hunted for contraband. Contraband could be pills, but it could also be a metal teaspoon, or a glass, or an electric kettle, or an electronic device.

The regime's dogs fed on humiliation. If their eyes fell upon you for some reason, and they took a dislike to a movement you made or the way you looked, they could make an example out of you in front of everyone, and when that happened, you had to submit, because any hint of resistance was a provocation. Your resistance signaled that there was something inside you that wasn't broken yet, and their job was to break it. Your chance of winning was zero.

There are all kinds of rabid dogs in this falling-apart wreck of a country. Usually it's freshly graduated police lieutenants, or officers in the criminal investigations units. But it could be any crazy fucker with a gun. The sense of terror the dogs provoke doesn't go away. It's still with me.

I learned a lesson that day, but that didn't stop me from forgetting it again, later, in the Khalifa precinct where I was transferred shortly before my release. A lieutenant and one of the crazy-fucker type of officers came in and ordered us to stand facing the wall with our hands up. For some reason I just couldn't stop myself from glancing out of the corner of my eye at the lieutenant as he made his way to the cell. The smack to my face came out of nowhere. He dragged me backward away from the wall, then pushed me forward so I smashed heavily into it, then did the same thing twice more, cursing the whole time. I made myself still and didn't resist at all, didn't let my face show any reaction, didn't even reach up to gently finger my raw and swollen forehead. That was the humiliation. And it worked. The officer moved on, and slapped another prisoner who was standing with his weight on one leg.

It happened again at the last stop before my release, Bulaq precinct, when a lieutenant—another fresh graduate—caught me smoking. He opened the wire mesh door and whacked me in the face, then dragged me, shaking and apologizing, out of the cell. I remember thinking at the time: I'm not going to write about this. I'm not going to tell anyone. If I do, I'll make it a black comedy. I'll add preposterous hyperbole for extra laughs, and shoehorn in some dramatic conflict between the social classes who are imprisoned cheek by jowl in cramped cells. How do you even write about being humiliated without making yourself the heroic underdog? The sense of abasement I feel is too bitter to become melodrama, I thought. When you're humiliated and broken, writing won't fix it.

When they finally let us go back to the cellblock, the entire contents of our cell were scattered on the ground. I found my clothes under a bag of tomatoes and cucumbers, and they'd confiscated our metal coffeepot and our improvised tuna-can ashtray. But they hadn't touched the books—or my manuscript.

ACKNOWLEDGMENTS

The Arabic original of this book would not have become what it is without the editorial input of Mohammad Rabie; discussions with Ahmad Nada, Hannah Elsisi, Mohamed Abdel Raouf, Ahmed Wael, Yasmine Omar, and Wael Abd El-Fattah, and their comments on earlier drafts; the assistance of the editors and copy editors at my publisher, Dar Sefsafa; and grants from the Arab Fund for Arts and Culture and the Andalus Institute for Tolerance and Anti-Violence Studies.

The English version owes a debt to the enthusiasm of Khaled Mattawa at the University of Michigan's creative writing program, who published several excerpts; to Katharine Halls's devoted translation of the book and her additional editorial advice; and to the editorial expertise of Daniel Gumbiner, who first worked on an excerpt published in *The Believer* magazine and later on the full text, and whose input opened my eyes to a new path that *Rotten Evidence* could take in its English incarnation.

My gratitude also goes to Beverly Rogers for her very generous support of the translation of this book, and of course to all my colleagues at the Black Mountain Institute and the City of Asylum Fellowship at the University of Nevada, Las Vegas for their support and above all for their friendship. A toast to that friendship!

From the early days of the court case which resulted in my conviction, and later, during my time in prison, and finally when I was released and went into exile, Alaa Abd el-Fattah was there. He is a part of the fabric of this book, and I owe him an enormous debt. As I write this, he is still in prison— but a prison much more vicious and cruel than the one I have described here. He has been deprived of music, of books, of the right to see his son, and of the comforts of friendship and human contact.

Along with Alaa, there are tens of thousands of others incarcerated in Egypt's prisons. This book is dedicated to them, in the hope that one day we all will be free and happy.

#FreeAlaa
#FreeThemAll

AHMED NAJI is a writer, journalist, documentary filmmaker, and criminal. His novel *Using Life* (2014) made him the first writer in Egyptian history to be imprisoned for offending public morality. He is also the author of the novels *Tigers, Uninvited* (2020) and *Happy Endings* (2022). Naji has won several prizes, including a Dubai Press Club Arab Journalism Award and a PEN/Barbey Freedom to Write Award. He was a City of Asylum Fellow at the Beverly Rogers, Carol C. Harter Black Mountain Institute in Las Vegas, where he still lives with his family. For more about his work, visit ahmednaji.net.